SIMPSONS COMICS

JAM-PACKED JAMBOREE

Harper

An Imprint of
HarperCollins*Publishers*

SIMPSONS COMICS JAM-PACKED JAMBOREE

HarperCollins books may be purchased for educational, business, or sales
promotional use. For information please write
Special Markets Department,
HarperCollins Publishers,
10 East 53rd Street, New York, NY 10022.

FIRST EDITION

ISBN-10: 0-06-087661-1
ISBN-13: 978-0-06-087661-6

06 07 08 09 10 QWM 10 9 8 7 6 5 4 3 2 1

Publisher: MATT GROENING
Creative Director: BILL MORRISON
Managing Editor: TERRY DELEGEANE
Director of Operations: ROBERT ZAUGH
Art Director: NATHAN KANE
Art Director Special Projects: SERBAN CRISTESCU
Production Manager: CHRISTOPHER UNGAR
Legal Guardian: SUSAN A. GRODE

Trade Paperback Concepts and Design: SERBAN CRISTESCU

Contributing Artists:
KAREN BATES, TIM BAVINGTON, JOHN COSTANZA, LEA HERNANDEZ, JASON HO, NATHAN KANE,
OSCAR GONZALEZ LOYO, BILL MORRISON, KEVIN M. NEWMAN, PHYLLIS NOVIN, PHIL ORTIZ, RICK REESE,
MIKE ROTE, HORACIO SANDOVAL, STEVE STEERE, JR., CHRIS UNGAR, ART VILLANUEVA

Contributing Writers:
IAN BOOTHBY, ABBY DENSON, CHUCK DIXON, DAN FYBEL
JESSE LEON MCCANN, GAIL SIMONE

PRINTED IN CANADA

WILDERNESS GUIDE

THAT'S THE SENTENCE I *WISH* I COULD GIVE YOU DEADBEAT DADS!

BUT SINCE THIS IS A *SMALL CLAIMS TV COURT*, I FINE YOU $400.

HEH, HEH! I LOVE HOW JUDGE JULIE GOES AFTER *LOUSY FATHERS* WHO DON'T GIVE THEIR KIDS WHAT THEY *NEED*.

I STILL GET THE $500 FEE FOR APPEARING ON THE SHOW, RIGHT?

IX-NAY ON THE EE-FAY!

DAD, I NEED *GLASSES*!

HERE'S A PAIR I FOUND IN FLANDERS' TRASH!

WHAT'CHA GOT, LIS? LAZY EYE?

HARDLY. I HAVE WHAT MY OPTOMETRIST CALLS *OVERACHIEVING EYE*.

DAD, I CAN'T WEAR *SOMEONE ELSE'S* GLASSES.

LISA, WE COULD FIGHT ALL DAY ABOUT THIS, OR WE COULD ASK THE *MAGIC ANSWER BOX*.

YOU MEAN THE *TV*?

SHHHH! IT'S *TALKING*.

HI, EVERYBODY!

HI, DR. NICK!

WELCOME TO MY PHONE IN SHOW WHERE I ANSWER ALL YOUR QUESTIONS ABOUT *MEDICALNESS* AND *DOCTOROLOGY*.

UH... DR. NICK?

SORRY.

NURSE SAMSON, PLEASE! I'M TRYING TO HOST A SHOW HERE.

BEEEEEEEEEEEEEEP!

CALLER ONE, YOU ARE ON THE AIR!

HELLO, DR. NICK, I HAVE A QUESTION ABOUT GLASSES FOR MY DAUGHTER. ARE ALL PRESCRIPTIONS THE SAME?

EXCUSE ME. NURSE, COULD YOU TURN THAT HEART MONITOR OFF? THAT *LONG SUSTAINED BEEP* IS SO *ANNOYING* TO THE *EAR HOLES*!

BEEEEEEEEEEEEEEEEEEP!

BUT BACK TO YOUR QUESTION. YES, ALL PRESCRIPTIONS ARE THE SAME. JUST LIKE DAILY WEAR THROWAWAY CONTACT LENSES WERE THE SAME AS THE REGULAR KIND.

IT'S ALL A BIG *EYE DOCTOR* SCAM.

SPEAKING OF SCAMS. FUNNY STORY. IT ALSO TURNS OUT *ALL KNOWN DISEASES* CAN BE CURED BY A SIMPLE *HOUSE-HOLD PRODUCT*.

I GUESS I COULD AT LEAST *TRY* MR. FLANDERS' GLASSES.

AAAAAH!

IT'S LIKE MY EYES WERE SOAKED IN *SUGAR!*

WHAT'S ALL THE *YELLING?* DID NEW ZEALAND INVADE? I TRIED TO WARN THE PRESIDENT, BUT WOULD HE LISTEN?

SOCIAL

OH, HI, GRAMPA. I'M YELLING BECAUSE I NEED GLASSES FOR ONE OF MY EYES.

I MIGHT BE ABLE TO HELP.

YEP, *HERE* IT IS!

A *MONOCLE?* DID YOU GET THIS FROM A *GERMAN OFFICER?*

KINDA. I *STOLE* IT FROM WERNER KLEMPERER'S DRESSING ROOM WHEN I WAS A *SECURITY GUARD* FOR TV'S "HOGAN'S HEROES."

OH MY GOSH! I CAN SEE *PERFECTLY.* THANKS, GRAMPA.

AS LONG AS IT'S AFTER *SCHOOL HOURS* OR ON *WEEKENDS*, I'LL DO IT!

YAY!

HUZZAH!

HOORAY!

BOOOOOOO!

WHAT?

THE NEXT DAY...

HEY, LISA! GIMME YOUR *LUNCH MONEY!*

I WILL NOT. I NEED THAT MONEY FOR A *WELL-BALANCED MEAL!*

O-OKAY LISA! WE DON'T WANT ANY *TROUBLE!* LET'S GET OUTTA HERE!

HMMMMM.

MEANWHILE...

NOW, SOME OF YOU MAY BE ASKING WHY WE'RE IN *THE MALL FOOD COURT.* THE *REAL* COURT WAS RENTED OUT FOR *BINGO* THIS WEEK, AND WE COULDN'T AFFORD TO GIVE THE DEPOSIT BACK.

FIRST UP, SNAKE. YOU ARE ACCUSED OF *CAR THEFT.* HOW DO YOU PLEAD?

I'VE *NEVER* STOLEN A CAR IN MY LIFE, DUDE!

THEN WHY ARE YOU *MR. JUNE* IN THE NEW *CAR THIEF SWIMSUIT CALENDAR?*

MMMM...MMMM. HE'S *GRAND THEFT AUTO-EROTIC!*

13

I'M SICK OF THE TAXPAYERS FOOTING THE BILL FOR YOUR TIME IN JAIL.

I SENTENCE YOU TO *RECESS* AT THE SPRINGFIELD ELEMENTARY GYMNASIUM.

HUH?

A SHORT SCHOOL BUS RIDE LATER...

SNAKE, I'D LIKE YOU TO MEET ALL THE PEOPLE WHOSE CARS YOU'VE STOLEN OVER THE YEARS.

LIKE, HI!

BRING OUT THE *DODGE BALLS*.

DUDE?

LET RECESS BEGIN!

LIKE, OW!

PTANG! THWOCK!

BAM!

Springfield Shopper

JUDGE SKINNER'S METHODS PRAISED BY ALL

EXCEPT HIS MOTHER WHO HAS "ISSUES"

LISA'S **HALLOWEEN CANDY** MUST BE AROUND HERE SOMEWHERE.

LET'S SEE, IF I WAS A **VEGETARIAN, STRAIGHT "A", JAZZ FAN**, WHERE WOULD I **HIDE** MY ALMOND JOYS AND SNICKER-DOODLES?

AHEM!

¡GASP!¡

OH, HI, LISA. I WAS JUST...

...REMAKING YOUR BED. THOSE HOSPITAL CORNERS CAN'T BE TOO TIGHT, YOU KNOW.

WELL, GOTTA GO.

LEAP!

WHAAAA?

AAAAAAAAAH!

DAD SAWED OFF THE **ESCAPE BRANCH** FROM THE TREE LAST SUMMER, REMEMBER?

OH, RIGHT.

THE NEXT DAY...

GET YOUR *FREE SAMPLE* OF OUR NEW ORGANIC FRUIT SNACKS!

I'D LIKE AN ORGANIC FRUIT SNACK.

TAKE THEM ALL, JUST DON'T *HURT ME!*

THIS MONOCLE SEEMS TO BRING WITH IT *RESPECT* AND *FEAR*. BUT I CAN'T LET IT *GO TO MY HEAD.*

I WANT FREE SAMPLES, AND I WANT THEM *NOW!*

YES, MA'AM!

SNAP!

WE'LL BE *BROADCASTING* YOUR NEXT FEW CASES *LIVE* ON THE NEWS, TO SEE IF YOU'RE READY TO HAVE YOUR OWN *TV SERIES.*

LIKE JUDGE JULIE?

HER SHOW'S BEEN PUT ON *HIATUS.*

"SHE WAS DETAINED IN TIJUANA FOR REASONS I'M NOT AT LIBERTY TO DISCUSS."

OKAY, OKAY. LET'S MAKE SURE WE GET OUR STORIES STRAIGHT.

YOU *STILL* WANT TO *MARRY ME*, RIGHT, KRUSTY?

I SURE DO! A WIFE CAN'T *TESTIFY* AGAINST HER HUSBAND *HERE*, TOO. *RIGHT?!!*

SERGIO ESTUVO AQUI!

XXX

YOU STOP BOTHERING JUDGE SKINNER, RIGHT NOW!

OR WHAT?

OR I'LL SHOW YOUR *BABY PICTURES* TO THE TV CAMERAS UNTIL YOU STOP!

NOOOOOO!

IT'S OVER! I'M DONE! I *APOLOGIZE* FOR THIS *HORRIBLE MISUNDERSTANDING.* JUST PUT THE PICTURES *AWAY!*

WELL DONE, WELL DONE. HUMILIATION, JUSTICE, PLUS A *TOUCH OF NUDITY.* I *LOVE IT!*

I WANT TO OFFER YOU YOUR *OWN SHOW* AS A *TV JUDGE.*

A JUDGE? I DON'T KNOW. I'VE BEEN ARRESTED... *TWICE.* IN FACT, *EVERY MEMBER* OF MY FAMILY *HAS,* EXCEPT FOR MAGGIE BECAUSE SHE WAS TOO YOUNG TO BE TRIED FOR *ATTEMPTED MURDER.*

I LOVE IT! IT GIVES YOU AN *EDGE.*

BUT WHAT ABOUT ME?

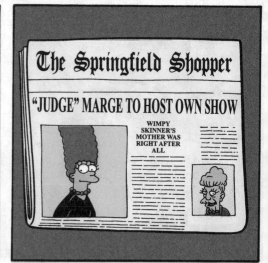

The Springfield Shopper

"JUDGE" MARGE TO HOST OWN SHOW

WIMPY SKINNER'S MOTHER WAS RIGHT AFTER ALL

19

YOU KNOW, I REALLY WOULD LIKE TO GET OUT OF HERE *EARLY* AND GET MY GROCERY SHOPPING DONE. WOULD YOU MIND CONFESSING? IT'D REALLY *HELP ME OUT*.

I DON'T WANNA.

CAN YOU REALLY LOOK *BAILIFF MAGGIE* IN THE EYE AND SAY YOU DIDN'T ROB THAT BANK?

I DID IT! I DID IT!

USING BABIES FOR CONFESSIONS.

WHEN I THINK OF ALL THE TIME I WASTED WITH PHONEBOOKS, RUBBER HOSES, AND PILLOW CASES FULL OF SOAP BARS.

WAY TO GO, JUDGE MARGE!

YAY!

MEANWHILE...

IF IT PLEASES THE COURT, I'D LIKE TO SUBMIT THESE PHOTOS AS EXHIBIT "A".

SO ENTERED.

THESE PHOTOS CLEARLY SHOW ONE HOMER J. SIMPSON *STEALING MY DESSERT!*

WHY YOU LITTLE...!

I WARNED YOU, MR. SIMPSON! ONE MORE *CHOKING RELATED OUTBURST,* AND YOU'D BE HELD IN CONTEMPT!

BUT THE BOY...

≶GAAK!≶

TAKE HIM AWAY!

WHERE DID *YOU* COME FROM?

TEMP AGENCY.

≶SIGH≶ I MISS MARGE.

FOR BREAKING AND ENTERING PLUS MAKING THE BAILIFF CRY, I GROUND YOU FOR TWO YEARS! NO DESSERTS OR CABLE TV!

I THINK YOU NEED A *TIME OUT* TO THINK ABOUT WHAT YOU'VE DONE.

NO! JUST SEND ME TO *PRISON!*

ORDER IS BEING MAINTAINED. EXCELLENT. NOW FOR A GOOD TOOTH BRUSHING AND THEN TO THE MALL.

I'LL JUST TAKE OUT THE MONOCLE, AND...

WHAT?

NO!

NEVER TAKE IT OUT! THE MONOCLE IS FEAR! THE MONOCLE IS POWER!

BUT, DO I WANT PEOPLE TO FEAR ME?

DUH! LOOK AT ALL THE STUFF YOU GOT TODAY! AND THERE'S MORE TO COME!

HOW MUCH MORE?

NO! THIS IS WRONG! THE POWER IS CORRUPTING ME!

THIS ENDS NOW!

NOOOOOOO!

LISA, GREAT NEWS! THE WERNER KLEMPERER FAN CLUB CALLED ME. THEY'RE OFFERING $50,000 FOR THE MONOCLE.

D'OH!

LATER THAT NIGHT AT THE (FOOD) COURT...

CAN'T WE WRAP IT UP NOW? I'M EXHAUSTED AND I MISS MY FAMILY.

NO! WE OWN YOU, MARGE. IN FACT, WE'D LIKE YOU TO START SLEEPING IN YOUR TRAILER INSTEAD OF GOING HOME AT NIGHT.

NOW FOR THE NEXT CASE...

WHAT THE...

MARGE, HONEY, WE NEED YOU BACK!

THE PLACE IS A *MESS*. I'M UNDER *HOUSE ARREST* AND CAN'T LEAVE HOME WITHOUT WEARING THIS *LEG BAND* THAT SHOCKS ME EVERY TWENTY SECONDS.

AAAAAH!

BART'S RUNNING THINGS, AND LISA'S UNDER A MONOCLE'S *EVIL POWER*.

NO, I'M NOT. I GOT OVER THAT *THIS AFTERNOON*.

WELL, THANKS FOR *KEEPING ME IN THE LOOP*. NOW I LOOK LIKE AN *IDIOT*.

AAAAAH!

OH, HOMER! I WISH I *COULD* QUIT, BUT THEY HAVE ME UNDER *CONTRACT*. THEY COULD *SUE*!

UM...MOM, YOU SIGNED THIS CONTRACT "JUDGE MARGE." IF YOU'RE NOT A JUDGE ANYMORE, IT'S *NOT VALID*.

I QUIT!

RRIP!

WAIT! YOU CAN'T!

BUT ONE FINAL *JUDICIAL ACT*! YOU'RE HELD *IN CONTEMPT* UNTIL I'M GONE!

COME ALONG YOU!

ALL RIGHT!

WAY TO GO MARGE!

NOW, LET'S ALL GET SOME ICE CREAM!

YAY!

SO, JUDGE SNYDER'S BEING REINSTATED RIGHT NOW?

YEP, AND AS A FORMER JUDGE, I HAVE A *GET OUT OF JAIL FREE CARD.*

OH, HOW CUTE. LIKE MONOPOLY. HEY, WAIT! THIS IS *REAL.*

AAAAAH!

ARE YOU OKAY, HOMEY?

YEAH, THE *POLICE* SAID THEY'D TAKE THE LEG BAND OFF WITHIN *FIVE BUSINESS DAYS.* THE ICE CREAM STOPS THE *INTERNAL ELECTRICAL BURNS* PRETTY GOOD, THOUGH.

AAAAAH!

WELL, YOU KNOW WHAT THEY SAY. "I SCREAM, YOU SCREAM, WE ALL SCREAM FOR ICE CREAM." HEE, HEE!

C'MON, MOM. DAD'S REALLY *SUFFERING.*

YOU'RE RIGHT. I'M SORRY.

AAAAAH!

HA! HA! HA! HA! HA!

THE END

ASTRONAUT STACY™!

CHEERLEADER STACY™!

NEUROSURGEON STACY™!

SUPREME COURT JUSTICE STACY™!

Malibu Mail!

Send all letters to:
Malibu Mail,
c/o Petrochem
Petrochemical Corporation
Springfield, USA

Well, we've got lots of letters in our mailbag this month, so let's get right to them, shall we?

Dear Malibu Stacy,
Congratulations on another fabulous issue. I must admit, the suspense when Malibu Tad asked you if you'd go to the big dance was unbearable! Kudos to the entire crew at *Malibu Stacy Comics* for their masterful story-telling.

However, I do have one small complaint...on page one of *"Stacy's Beach Brunch Bunch,"* the dots on her fashionable two-piece swimsuit are light red--and yet, just a page later, they're dark pink. How could this be?

I'm pleasingly puzzled!

Your biggest fan,
Waylon Smithers

Well, I must say, you certainly ARE a sharp-eyed little girl! However, it's easy to explain. I got a little bit of nasty ol' sand on my suit, so, of course, I had to run and change! But thanks for paying such close attention to my stories, and congratulations to your parents for giving you such an unusual and charming name!

Dear Malibu Stacy,
I'm in fourth grade. There's this boy I like, but I'm not sure if he likes me. What should I do?

Tina Pemberton

This one's easy! Simply find out what this boy likes, and completely change your likes and personality to match his. Some of the best solutions are the simplest ones! Let me know how it turns out, Tina!

Dear Malibu Stacy,
I'm eight years old, and I go to Springfield Elementary. I love your adventures and your carefree attitude. I've drawn a picture of you, which I've included.

Lisa Simpson

P.S. If this is considered trespassing on your copyrighted image, please forgive me, as I am unaware of the legal consequences.

Dear Lisa,

I would never wear green with orange.

Well, that's all for this month! Join us next month for my next thrilling adventure, "Never Enough Shoes!"

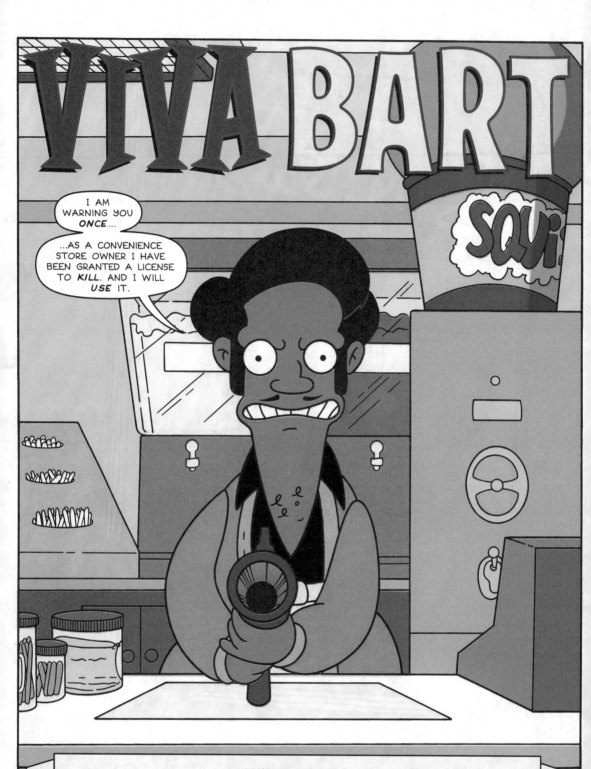

VIVA BART

I AM WARNING YOU *ONCE*...

...AS A CONVENIENCE STORE OWNER I HAVE BEEN GRANTED A LICENSE TO *KILL*. AND I WILL *USE* IT.

CHUCK DIXON
STORY

HORACIO SANDOVAL
PENCILS

ART VILLANUEVA
COLORS

STEVE STEERE, JR.
INKS

KAREN BATES
LETTERS

BILL MORRISON
EDITOR

MATT GROENING
BENEVOLENT DICTATOR

HAND IT OVER!

NO *WAY!*

GIMME!

UNNH–UH!

HELLO? AGITATED CONVENIENCE STORE OWNER WITH *ITCHY TRIGGER FINGER?* NEED I SAY MORE?

BUT IT'S THE *LAST* SIX PACK OF DUFF, APU!

AND *I* SAW IT FIRST.

I MUST BLAME *MYSELF,* LOYAL CUSTOMERS.

I UNDERESTIMATED THE *THIRST* OF THE *TEACHER'S UNION* CONVENTION MEETING IN TOWN THIS WEEK.

I GUESS WE *COULD* SPLIT IT...

SURE, WE'RE *PALS,* HOMER.

BARNEY! LOOK!

THE *DUFF* TRUCK!

SWEET *DELIVERANCE!*

WHERE *IS* IT?

¡YOINK!¡

ONE SIX PACK TO *GO,* APU!

HA HA HA!

NO

YOU'LL BE *SORRY,* HOMER!

DON'T *THINK* SO!

HEE HEE HEE HEE HEE!

YOU WON'T *ENJOY* THAT BEER! IT'LL BRING YOU NOTHING BUT *MISERY!* IT'LL BE FLAT AND TASTELESS, AND YOU'LL *REGRET* THIS DAY!

ITS FOAMY GOODNESS WILL TURN TO *POISON* IN YOUR MOUTH.

GUG GUG GUG GUG

MMM...PURE AMBROSIA.
MAN, NOTHING ON TV. SUNDAY AFTER-NOONS BITE.
HEY, HOMER. YOU SEE THIS CONTEST? TWO WEEKS IN A TROPICAL PARADISE.
YOU DRAIN PLENTY OF BREWSKIS. MAYBE YOU COULD WIN.
DUFF'S CARIBBEAN ESCAPE! YOU COULD BE A WINNER!
Duff Beer
Duff BEER
NAW...THOSE CONTESTS ARE ALL SO PHONY. NOBODY ACTUALLY WINS THEM.
WHAT KIND OF LOSER BUYS BEER JUST TO WIN A CONTEST?
AWW...
NO BALMY TROPICAL BREEZES FOR GIL...
Be a Winner

SOON...

DUFF BEER IS *PROUD* TO ANNOUNCE THE WINNER OF OUR *CARIBBEAN ESCAPE!*

A MAN WHO *KNOWS* THE FROSTY AMBER GOODNESS OF DUFF AND DRINKS A *LOT* OF IT!

THAT'S *ME!*

YOU AND YOUR FAMILY WILL SPEND TWO WEEKS ON *SANDY BEACHES* UNDER A *TROPICAL SUN* THANKS TO *DUFF!*

WOW. *BIG* TICKETS.

TO SYMBOLIZE THE BIG *FUN* YOU'LL BE HAVING!

BOSQUEVERDE? BUT ISN'T THAT PLACE A GODAWFUL--

--FULLY *WONDERFUL* PARADISE ISLAND OF BEAUTY AND JOY?

YOU *BET,* LITTLE GIRL!

WHO *SAYS* DRINKING BEER TO WIN A CONTEST MAKES YOU A LOSER?

YOU DID, DAD.

IN YOUR *FACE!*

Dear Diary,
While everyone else enjoys the hospitality of our despotic host, I choose to explore Bosqueverde's natural splendor.

This is nature undisturbed by man or mini-mall.

AH.

I'll have to look this woodland friend up in "Little Ms. Know-it-all's Book of Creatures".

RARRRRRRR!

YAAAAAAH!

?

In fact, I think I'll go get that book right away.

OH, NO!

GENETICALLY-ALTERED FOOD!

STOP! ¡ALTO!

CUT IT OUT!

THINK ABOUT WHAT YOU'RE DOING! YOU'RE DESECRATING MOTHER NATURE'S PLANS AND RISKING A GENETIC HOLOCAUST WITH THESE SCIENTIFIC MOCKERIES OF THE EARTH'S BOUNTY!

SHE HAS SEEN THE BANANAS GIGANTES!

SHE CANNOT BE ALLOWED TO ESCAPE!

WELL...AH... ¡ADIÓS!

¡NIÑA IDIOTA!

GET HER!

¡WHEW! LOST THEM.

FOR A DEVELOPING NATION THIS PLACE IS PRETTY LAME.

WHERE'S THE CONSCIENCE OF BOSQUEVERDE?

SO, THERE'S *SOME* HOPE AFTER ALL.

¡NO HAY PA

¡VAMOS! ¡ÁNDALE!
THE PEOPLE'S REVOLUTIONARY PEOPLE'S ARMY OF BOSQUEVERDE

THIS IS A SMOKE-FREE JUNGLE

MEAN PEOPLE SUCK
FUR IS MURDER
AMERICAN POP STARS WELCOME.

KLAK! SHAK!

OOP.

K-KLAK!

SNIK!

LOOK, I'M ON *YOUR* SIDE. REALLY!

I *APPRECIATE* THAT YOU WANT TO STICK IT TO THE MAN.

MOVE ALONG, BLONDIE.

I AM COMANDANTE W.

DOUBLE-U?

ALL THE *GOOD* LETTERS WERE TAKEN.

WE FIGHT FOR FREEDOM AND THE RIGHT TO VOTE FOR ME. SO, YOU ARE *SIMPÁTICA* WITH OUR CAUSE.

AS LONG AS IT'S ABOUT JUSTICE FOR ALL LIVING THINGS.

SOMETHING LIKE THAT. THERE ARE *OTHER* AMERICANOS HERE AS WELL.

KRIS KRISTOFFERSON.

VIVA LA REVOLUCIÓN, MI AMIGA.

SHERYL CROW.

NICE TO SEE YOU.

ALEC BALDWIN.

I'VE **GOT** TO STOP SAYING I'LL LEAVE THE COUNTRY EVERY TIME SOMEONE I DON'T LIKE RUNS FOR OFFICE.

THE GUY WHO PLAYED URKEL.

WHAT CAN I **SAY**? IT'S A **GIG**.

I HATE TO **SAY** THIS, BUT EVEN FOR A GUERILLA LAIR THIS IS PRETTY LOW RENT.

TELL ME ABOUT IT. IF NOT FOR THE MONEY FROM TED TURNER, WE WOULD BE IN EVEN WORSE SHAPE.

AND EVEN **HE** MAKES DEMANDS OF US.

WHAT WE NEED ARE **FRESH** IDEAS FOR DISRUPTING GENERAL HIDALGO'S PUPPET STATE.

IDEAS THAT DO NOT REQUIRE MUCH **CASH** OUTLAY.

COMANDANTE, I MAY HAVE THE SOLUTION TO **ALL** YOUR PROBLEMS.

BART?

BART?

BART!

BART, IT'S *ME*!

AYE CARUMBA!

WATCH YOUR LANGUAGE IN FRONT OF MY *NIÑO*!

OW!

SLAP!

WHAT'D I SAY?

HEY, WHERE'VE YOU *BEEN*, LIS'? *MOM* WAS LOOK-ING FOR YOU.

NO TIME FOR THAT. LISTEN *UP*, BART. THIS MAY BE THE OPPORTUNITY OF A *LIFETIME*.

LET ME GET THIS *STRAIGHT*...

YOU WANT ME TO HELP YOU PLAY MINDLESS PRANKS AND POSSIBLY DANGEROUS PRACTICAL JOKES TO DISRUPT THE STATUS QUO OF YOUR WHOLE *COUNTRY*?

JUST THINK OF GENERAL HIDALGO AS PRINCIPAL SKINNER.

TEMPTING... TEMPTING...

49

REVOLUTION FOR THE *HELL* OF IT?

SIGN ME *UP!*

¡GENERAL!

THE PRESIDENT OF THE UNITED STATES IS ON THE PHONE!

I'LL TAKE IT ON LINE TWO.

SEÑOR PRESIDENTE, HOW MAY I *ASSIST* YOU?

I'M LOOKING FOR ONE OF MY AMBASSADORS.

ALLOW ME TO *HELP.*

HER NAME IS *MARY COHEN.*

I SHALL *ASK* FOR HER.

POR FAVOR. HAS ANY ONE SEEN MARY COHEN?

I AM *LOOKING* FOR A MARY COHEN. WILL SOMEONE FIND A *MARY COHEN* FOR ME?

WHAT IS SO *HUMOROSO?*

¡SNORT!¿

MARICON... ¿GIGGLE¿.*

*MARICON=SISSY

WHERE *IS* THIS MARY COHEN I SEEK?

HA! HA! HA! HA! HA! HA! HA! HA! HA! HA! HA!

THE PSYCHOLOGICAL PHASE OF MY ATTACK HAS BEGUN.

NOW WE GET *SERIOUS.*

YOU SAY YOU ARE WILLING TO *TELL* ME THE IDENTITY OF THIS VANDAL WHO PLAGUES MY EVERY WAKING MOMENT?

AND WHAT DO YOU WISH IN *RETURN*...

...SEÑOR *SKINNER*?

NOT A *THING*, GENERAL, SO LONG AS YOU *KEEP* HIM IN YOUR COUNTRY UNTIL HE'S EIGHTEEN.

THIS TOMFOOLERY HAS ALL THE EARMARKS OF ONE BART SIMPSON OF SPRINGFIELD, U.S.A.

SO, OUR GUESTS HAVE GONE FROM TOURIST TO *TERRORIST*.

I WANT THEM TO BE *FOUND* AND TO MEET WITH AN UNFORTUNATE AND *HORRIFYING* ACCIDENT!

MOM!

MOM!

WHAT *IS* IT, KIDS?

LISA GOT ME TO JOIN SOME REBEL FRIENDS OF HERS, AND NOW THE ARMY HAS ORDERS TO SHOOT TO *KILL* ME.

IT'S *TRUE*, MOM! BART MAY HAVE ACTUALLY *OVER-ACHIEVED* THIS TIME.

WELL, I GUESS WE'LL HAVE TO GET YOUR *FATHER* AND SEE ABOUT LEAVING.

YOU WIN *AGAIN*, SEÑOR SIMPSON.

I AM *NEVER* LEAVING THIS PLACE!

LOOK AT ALL THIS *MOOLAH*!

YOU HAVE WON *EIGHTEEN MILLION* BOSQUEVERDAN *CHU-CHUS.*

HOW MUCH IS IT IN *AMERICAN*?

I SHALL *CALCULATE* IT, SEÑOR.

HOMER, WE'RE ALL IN GREAT *DANGER*!

WE GOTTA LEAVE *NOW*, DAD!

WHAT? AND LEAVE A *FORTUNE* BEHIND?

IT IS *SIX DOLLARS AND TWENTY-NINE CENTS* IN YOUR DOLLARS, SEÑOR.

SEE?

THERE THEY ARE!

ALL BETTING IS CLOSED UNTIL THE EXECUTION IS OVER.

WE HAVE TO *RUN*, DAD!

MY FAMILY IS GOING TO BE MURDERED...AND ON *FAJITAS NIGHT*!

BLAM!

BLAM!

THE NORTEAMERICANOS ARE TO BE *BUTCHERED* BY OUR OPPRESSORS!

THIS IS THE MOMENT WE HAVE *WAITED* FOR.

YES! THEY WILL MAKE A *TELEVISION* MOVIE ABOUT THIS!

BY FEBRUARY SWEEPS WE COULD BE *FREE*!

WATCH NCAA ACTION ON **TNT**

¡ALTO, GRINGOS!

YOU WILL STAND STILL TO BE SHOT, POR FAVOR.

EEP!

WHUPPA!

WHUPPA!

BRRRRRRRT!

IF WE GET GUNNED DOWN IN A HAIL OF HOT LEAD, YOU ARE IN *BIG* TROUBLE, BOY!

SORRY, HOMESLICE!

INTO THE *JUNGLE!* WE CAN *HIDE* THERE!

WHERE'S FLANDERS' WEED-WHACKER WHEN WE *NEED* IT?

IT'S AT HOME IN OUR *GARAGE*.

STUPID *FLANDERS!* WHAT GOOD IS IT DOING US *THERE?*

STOP RIGHT THERE!

GAAAAAAAH!

TAKE THE *BOY! HE* DID IT!

GOOD AH-FTERNOON. I AM *RAINIER WOLFCASTLE,* CURRENTLY FILMING "MCBAIN XII: THE DAY AFTER THE LAST DAY ON EARTH." WE NEED *EX*-TRAHS TO PLAY TERRIFIED AH-MERICAN HOSTAGES.

SHOW US TO OUR *TRAILER,* MR. WOLFCASTLE!

WELL, IT LOOKS LIKE WE'RE GOING HOME.

I CAN'T *WAIT,* MARGE. THIS IS THE WORST VACATION *EVER.* IT'S LIKE I'VE BEEN *CURSED!*

HEH HEH HEH HEH HEH

HEH HEH HEH HEH HEH HEH

QUIT THAT MANIACAL LAUGHTER, BARNEY.

IT'S *CREEPIN'* ME OUT.

THE END

Beauty School HELLCATS

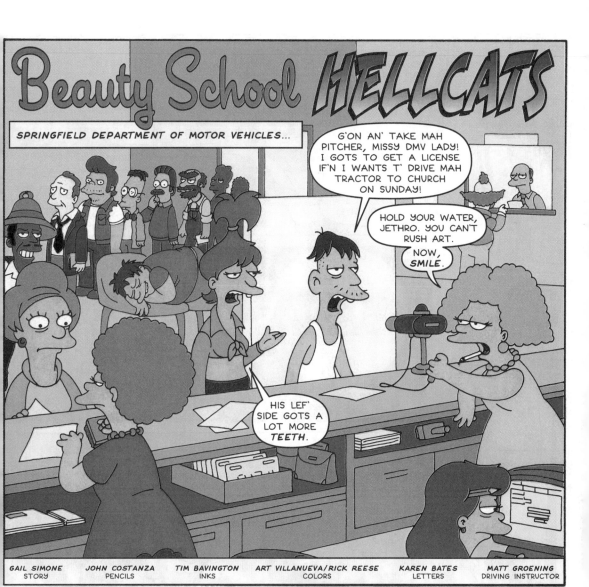

SPRINGFIELD DEPARTMENT OF MOTOR VEHICLES...

G'ON AN' TAKE MAH PITCHER, MISSY DMV LADY! I GOTS TO GET A LICENSE IF'N I WANTS T' DRIVE MAH TRACTOR TO CHURCH ON SUNDAY!

HOLD YOUR WATER, JETHRO. YOU CAN'T RUSH ART.

NOW, *SMILE*.

HIS LEF' SIDE GOTS A LOT MORE *TEETH*.

GAIL SIMONE STORY   **JOHN COSTANZA** PENCILS   **TIM BAVINGTON** INKS   **ART VILLANUEVA/RICK REESE** COLORS   **KAREN BATES** LETTERS   **MATT GROENING** DRIVING INSTRUCTOR

YA MEANS LIKE *THIS*?

UGH, *NO*.

DO YOU MIND IF I...?

WHUT TH'...?!!?

YOU *GO*, GAL!

JUST A LITTLE *TOUCH-UP* HERE AND THERE...

SELMA, DO YOU *LIKE* WORKING HERE?

OF COURSE NOT. I *HATE* IT HERE. IT'S *DEHUMANIZING* AND *SPIRIT-CRUSHING*.

GOOD, GOOD.

I'LL BE FRANK, SELMA. UP UNTIL RECENTLY, YOU'VE NEVER SHOWN AN *OUNCE* OF CREATIVITY, NOR HAVE YOU *EVER* PERFORMED YOUR WORK WITH THE SLIGHTEST ENTHUSIASM.

IN SHORT, YOU'VE BEEN A *PERFECT EMPLOYEE*.

SO, WHY NOT TAKE A NICE, *LONG* VACATION? FIND A WAY TO *RID* YOURSELF OF THESE..."*CREATIVE IMPULSES*."

PLEASE WAIT YOUR TURN TO BE FIRED! YOU ARE NUMBER:

41

BECAUSE IF YOU STILL *HAVE* THEM WHEN YOU COME BACK...I'M AFRAID YOU'LL HAVE TO TAKE A *NUMBER*.

HEY, WHERE ARE *YOU* GOING?

TO ENROLL IN BEAUTY SCHOOL, LIKE I'VE ALWAYS DREAMED!

HOT DOG! HANG ON, I'M COMING WITH YOU!

OH, MAN, I *KNEW* I SHOULDN'T HAVE DRAWN THAT AWESOME HOT ROD ON MY TEST FORM!

FAILED

WHAT ABOUT THE PEOPLE STILL IN LINE?

HEH. GOOD ONE. "WHAT ABOUT THE PEOPLE STILL IN LINE." HEH.

HEH. AHEH.

SOON...

PATTY, I CAN'T BELIEVE IT! I'M *FINALLY* GOING TO BEAUTY SCHOOL!

OUTDATED MAGAZINES AND UNLIMITED GOSSIP, *HERE WE COME!*

Mister Pierre's Academe of Beauty and Image
(Formerly Pete's Budget Bowl Cuts)

DAY THIRTY-SEVEN...

SELMA! THAT'S NOT HAIRSPRAY--IT'S PURE *PEROXIDE!*

DUDE, MY EYES ARE LIKE *TOTALLY* LIQUEFYING!

DAY SIXTY-FIVE...

YOU'RE *NEVER* GOING TO PASS THE PRACTICAL EXAM AT THIS RATE, BOUVIER! YOU SHOULD *DROP OUT IMMEDIATELY!*

≶SOB!≶

I GOT NO PLACE ELSE TO GO!

FINAL EXAM DAY...

THAT'S IT, PATTY. I CAN'T DO *ANYTHING* RIGHT HERE. I'LL *FAIL* FOR SURE, AND I'LL NEVER GET TO KNOW THE *JOY* OF HAVING MY OWN *CURLING IRON HOLSTER.*

BUT YOUR HAIR-CUTS AT THE *DMV* WERE SO *CREATIVE!*

THINK, WHAT DID YOU HAVE AT THE *DMV* THAT YOU CAN'T HAVE HERE?

NICOTINE, TAR AND *OTHER* TOXINS!!

NO TIME TO UNWRAP, JUST LIGHT THE *WHOLE PACK!*

AH, *THAT'S* THE STUFF!

NOW, LET ME AT THEM SCALPS! THEY NEED SOME *SELMA-GINATION!*

YOU'RE *LATE,* LADIES! YOUR *FINAL EXAM VOLUNTEERS* ARE WAITING!

NOW GO, BOTH OF YOU! GO AND *MAKE MR. PIERRE PROUD!* ≶SNIFF!≶

CONGRATULATIONS, SELMA. YOU'VE *EARNED* THIS DIPLOMA.

I...I NEVER WOULDA MADE IT IF NOT FOR YOU.

ARE YOU *SEEING* ANYONE CURRENTLY BY CHANCE?

:CHOKE: GET THE HELL OUT OF HERE.

I'M SO PROUD OF YOU BOTH! WHAT *NEXT*? ARE YOU GOING TO *OPEN* A SALON?

NO, MY DREAM CAME TRUE ALREADY. IT'S BACK TO THE *DMV* FOR US! THEY PROBABLY HAVE A LINE OF CUSTOMERS OUT THE DOOR BY NOW.

OH YEAH. WE'D BETTER HURRY. AHEH. HEH.

HEH. AHEH, HEH!

NEXT: LIZARD MAKEOVERS!

NO, I KEEP TELLING YOU! IT'S *MY* WIFE THAT PASSED AWAY!

WHICH IS WHY I'M TRYING TO GIVE YOU OUR TICKETS TO A *ROMANTIC COUPLES CRUISE* WE BOOKED A YEAR AGO.

DID YOU SAY A *CRUISE*?

ZZIP!

WELL, I'D LIKE TO GO, FLANDERS, BUT I'M *TERRIFIED OF WATER*.

THANK YOU, NED. WE'D BE HAPPY TO TAKE YOUR TICKETS.

SWIPE!

BUT MARGE.

OH, HOMER. JUST CALL UP DR. HIBBERT AND HAVE HIM CURE YOUR *RABIES*!

AND GET RID OF THAT RACCOON!

≀SOB!≀ GOODBYE, MR. NIBBLES!

THREE DAYS AND SEVERAL PAINFUL INJECTIONS LATER...

CAPTAIN McCALLISTER'S **CRUISING ADVENTURES!** NOT ASSOCIATED WITH THE AL PACINO FILM 'CRUISING'

WELCOME ABOARD YE' LANDLUBBIN' LOVEBIRDS!

CHECK IT OUT, MARGE! THE BARNACLES SMELL LIKE *POTPOURRI!*

NOW THAT'S CLASS!

OH, HOMER, LOOK AT THE POOL.

⧙YAWN⧘

OOOH, A *TRAINED DOLPHIN!*

EH!

AND IT'S *SERVING DRINKS.*

OUT OF MY WAY!

FINALLY, AN ANIMAL THAT DOES SOMETHING USEFUL BESIDES TASTE GOOD!

HEY, HOMER! WHERE DO YOU WANT THIS ICE FOR THE BAR DRINKS?

KERASH!

THE NEXT WEEK...

I WOULD LIKE TO *RETRACT* MY EARLIER STATEMENT ABOUT GOD AND HIS SHIP-SINKING ABILITIES. I'D ALSO LIKE TO TAKE THIS TIME TO *PRAISE* BUDDHA, ALLAH, AND, TO A LESSER EXTENT, RA!

GONE FISSION
HOMER'S SUPER BOAT

GIVE A GOOD WORD TO THE MAN UPSTAIRS FOR US, WOULD YOU, REVEREND?

WILL DO!

WELCOME ABOARD HOMER'S *SUPERBOAT CRUISELINE OF LOVE!*

SMILES EVERYONE! SMILES!

SO WHO ARE THESE COUPLES, HOMER?

WHAT DO YOU MEAN, BOY? YOU *KNOW* EVERYBODY.

MAYBE, I JUST LIKE HEARING EXPOSITION-STYLE CHARACTER DESCRIPTIONS, OKAY?

FINE, KNOCK YOURSELF OUT!

THERE'S PRINCIPAL SKINNER AND YOUR TEACHER MRS. KRABAPPEL. LOOKS LIKE HE'S BROUGHT HIS WORK WITH HIM, AND SHE'S NOT *TOO HAPPY* ABOUT IT.

THE NEWLY-DIVORCED LUANN VAN HOUTEN AND HER BOYFRIEND PYRO...

...AND THERE'S HER EX-HUSBAND, KIRK VAN HOUTEN, WHO'S WITH HIS *NEW GIRLFRIEND*, TENILLE.

WHERE'S SHE?

I CAN HEAR YOU, AND SHE'S RUNNING A BIT LATE, OKAY?

THERE'S APU AND MANJULA, RECENTLY BLESSED WITH *OCTUPLETS*.

HEY, HOMER, IMAGINE IF I WAS AN OCTUPLET. WOULDN'T THAT BE *COOL*?

≶SHUDDER.≷ THAT THOUGHT IS GONNA TAKE A LOT OF BEER TO WASH AWAY.

THE MILLIONAIRE AND HIS WIFE.

THE LAST TIME I *RELAXED* I ENDED UP IN A *P.O.W CAMP* EATING *DUNG BEETLES*.

ALWAYS WITH THE DUNG BEETLES.

AT LEAST TAKE OFF YOUR SUIT AND TIE.

FOR THE LAST TIME, NO!

HMMMF!

WELL, THAT'S GOING ON *HER* PERMANENT RECORD.

HOMER, I THINK PRINCIPAL SKINNER AND MRS. KRABAPPEL'S RELATIONSHIP IS IN *TROUBLE*.

RELAX, MARGE, I'VE SEEN EVERY EPISODE OF "THE LOVE BOAT" AND "THE NEW LOVE BOAT."

ALL A TROUBLED RELATIONSHIP NEEDS IS A *ZANY MISUNDER-STANDING*.

BUT...

OH, FIRST MATE BART?

SOON...

EDNA IS HAVING AN *AFFAIR* WITH *PYRO*?!!

TO THE BEST OF MY KNOWLEDGE, YES.

THAT NIGHT...

WHERE'S YOUR *GIRLFRIEND*, MR. VAN HOUTEN?

UH...SHE'S *SEA SICK.*

WELCOME TO THE *CAPTAIN'S TABLE*. RELAX, EAT AND LET THE *LOVE VIBES* FLOW.

PASS THE PEAS?

I GUESS HE'D KNOW ABOUT *MAKING PASSES.* RIGHT, EDNA?

CAN I HAVE THE HAM THEN?

WHAT?

WHY DON'T YOU CHEW ON THIS *KNUCKLE SANDWICH*, HOMEWRECKER!

SOCK!

WHAM!

JUST IGNORE THEM! THEY'RE JUST HAVING A BOUT OF *OCEAN MADNESS.* THEY'LL GET THEIR *SEA BRAINS* SOON!

GO ABOUT YOUR *LOVE TALK!*

:GASP!:

MANJULA, NO! **COME BACK!**

THAT GOT THE **OLD PASSION** BACK.

PYRO! I ATE MY ENTIRE DINNER **ALONE**. YOU PROMISED YOU WOULDN'T LET YOUR **LOVE OF BATTLE** INTERFERE WITH OUR LOVE.

THIS HAS NOTHING TO DO WITH MY "AMERICAN GLADIATOR" TRAINING. I...

MAYBE WHEN YOU'RE FINISHED PLAYING WITH **YOUR FRIEND,** YOU'LL HAVE TIME FOR ME.

YOU ONLY MARRIED ME FOR **MY MONEY!**

WELL, YOU ONLY MARRIED **ME** FOR **MY** MONEY!

OKAY, OKAY DON'T *PANIC.* WE'LL JUST GIVE THEM THE MILLIONAIRE'S MONEY, AND THEY'LL LEAVE US ALONE!

BUT WE DON'T HAVE ANY *REAL MONEY!*

WE'RE ⸬SOB⸬ *DOT COM MILLIONAIRES!*

PYRO! YOU CAN HELP US FIGHT THEM!

WHAT'S THE POINT? WITHOUT LOVE MY *FIGHTING SPIRIT* IS GONE!

WHAT DO YOU MEAN? YOU'VE GOT THE LOVE OF *TWO* WOMEN!

LUANN AND EDNA!

EDNA?

WHAT ARE YOU TALKING ABOUT? I LOVE *YOU,* NOT PYRO!

THEN YOU'RE *NOT* HAVING AN AFFAIR?

NO!

WELL GIVE ME A D- IN *CONDUCT* AND AN INCOMPLETE IN *COMMON SENSE.* I LOVE YOU TOO, EDNA.

DIVORCE US, HOMER.

DONE!

WHEW!

SO THAT'S WHY YOU WERE FIGHTING HIM? I'M SORRY FOR *SNAPPING* AT YOU. DARN THOSE *WINE SPRITZERS*. THEY TURN ME INTO A *BEAST*.

YOUR *PASSION* REMINDED ME WHY I FELL FOR YOU, LUANN VAN HOUTEN!

WELL, ALL THIS *MAKING UP* IS WELL AND GOOD FOR THE REST OF YOU, BUT WE ARE STILL NOT *MAN AND WIFE*, POSSIBLY.

AND THERE IS NOTHING ANY OF YOU CAN DO TO CHANGE THAT!

I'M CAPTAIN. YOU'RE *MARRIED*.

WELL, I CERTAINLY *SET MYSELF UP* FOR THAT!

I LOVE YOU, WIFE.

AND I YOU, HUSBAND.

AH...HAVE YOU ALL FORGOTTEN ABOUT THE PIRATES?

OH YOU'RE JUST *BITTER* BECAUSE YOUR GIRLFRIEND DOESN'T REALLY *EXIST*.

OH, YEAH. WELL, MAYBE YOUR BOYFRIEND DOESN'T EXIST, *EITHER!*

I'M RIGHT HERE.

YOU'VE WON *THIS ROUND*, LUANN!

WAIT A MINUTE! *THIS* PIRATE IS REALLY...

YANK!

CAPTAIN MCCALLISTER!

AAAR! I JUST WANTED TO RUIN YER' CRUISE LIKE *YOU* RUINED *MINE*. AND I WOULD HAVE GOTTEN AWAY WITH IT, TOO...

...IF I WERE *SMARTER*.

OH, KIRK! DID I *MISS* ANYTHING?

YOUR GIRL-FRIEND IS *REAL*?!

AND *REAL HOT!* RRRRRROWL!

YEAH! SHE'S REAL! SO *THERE!*

CAPTAIN? IS THAT YOU?

TENILLE?

WHAT THE...?

SHE'S MY DARLING WIFE I THOUGHT LOST AT SEA YEARS AGO!

WELL, I *DID* MEET HER THROUGH A LOST AT SEA *DATING SERVICE*.

SO ASIDE FROM KIRK, EVERY-ONE'S HAPPY AND IN LOVE!

I'M THE *BEST CRUISE GUY* EVER!

THE END

OH, IT'S *YOU!* AND YOU'RE *EARLY!*

LISTEN, I APPRECIATE THE EFFORT, BUT WE DON'T PAY MUCH ATTENTION TO OL' *MR. TIMECLOCK* HERE. YOU KNOW WHAT I MEAN?

NOPE, IT'S *PEOPLE* THAT COUNT, AND JUST BY LOOKING AT YOU, I CAN TELL YOU'RE DEFINITELY *PEOPLE*.

HEY, CAN I GET YOU ANYTHING?

OH, YOU *GOTTA* TRY THESE *SOY-POPS*. THESE ARE GONNA BE *HUGE* IN THE HEALTH SNACK MARKET... THEY'RE *DELICIOUS!*

I THINK I'LL HAVE ONE MYSELF!

OKAY, I'LL BE VERY HONEST WITH YOU. THAT WASN'T DELICIOUS AT ALL. THE BOYS IN R&D CAN BUILD A *LASER DEATH-TRAP* YOU WOULDN'T BELIEVE, BUT THEY CAN'T ENGINEER A DECENT *PINEAPPLE-FLAVORED SOY-POP*, BLESS THEIR HEARTS!

LISTEN, I'VE GOT A GOOD FEELING ABOUT YOU. JUST LET ME ASK, FOR THE *RECORD*...

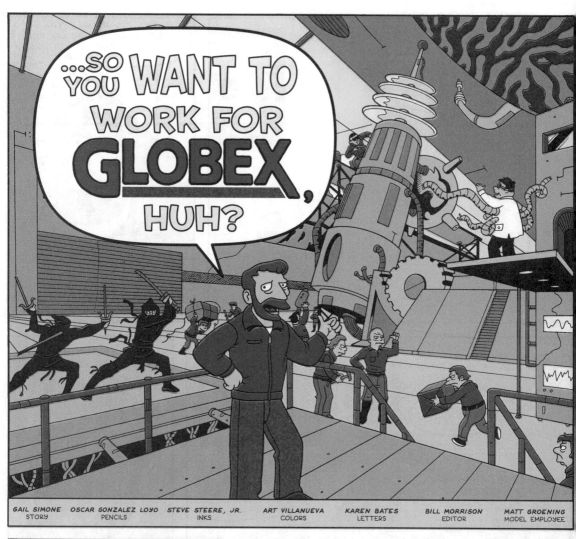

...SO YOU WANT TO WORK FOR **GLOBEX**, HUH?

GAIL SIMONE
STORY

OSCAR GONZALEZ LOYO
PENCILS

STEVE STEERE, JR.
INKS

ART VILLANUEVA
COLORS

KAREN BATES
LETTERS

BILL MORRISON
EDITOR

MATT GROENING
MODEL EMPLOYEE

WELL, WE *WANT* YOU TO. HONEST!

HEY, LET'S GO MEET SOME OF THE GUYS! WANT TO? OKAY, LET'S!

NOW, HERE'S A GREAT BUNCH OF GUYS. MEET *GENERAL CLAW, SCARFACE, KAHBLU KHAN,* AND *THE MONOCLE!*

HOWDY, NEW GUY!

CHARMED, I'M SURE.

I WEEL SLEET HEES THROAT!

OKAY, IT'S *NOT* CUTE. I ADMIT IT.

EXIT

SNAP!

NO POINT IN DENYING IT. SCARFACE HAS A BIT OF A *HOMICIDAL IMPULSE PROBLEM*, BUT HE'S A GOOD MAN, AND DARN IT, HE *KNOWS* HOW TO TRAIN A *GIANT WEASEL!*

LOOK, I CAN SEE YOU'RE A BIT *CONCERNED* ABOUT COMING TO *WORK* FOR ME, RIGHT?

WORRIED ABOUT GOING TO *PRISON*, I BET. WELL, LEMME *SHOW* YOU SOMETHING.

MULTI-MEDIA ROOM

YESTERDAY'S GLOBEX

STOCK MARKET TAMPERING
INDUSTRIAL SABOTAGE
INTERNATIONAL TERRORISM
ILLEGAL ARMS TRADING
COMIC BOOK COUNTERFEITING
TREASON
MILITARY ESPIONAGE
HABITUAL NAPSTER USAGE
GAME-SHOW FIXING

NOW, IT'S TRUE THAT IN THE PAST, MY COMPANY HAS BEEN INVOLVED IN SOME *QUESTIONABLE VENTURES*.

BUT, SEE, *TODAY'S* GLOBEX IS...

HEY, WHAT'S SO *FUNNY?*

TODAY'S GLOBEX!

HEALTH-FOOD MARKETING
NOVELTY SINGING FISH PRODUCTION
OSMOND SOUND-ALIKE RECORDING
BULK HYMNAL DISTRIBUTION
MAIL-ORDER WEDDING APPAREL

GLOBUL DOMINASHUN!

HA! HA! HA!
HAR! HAR!

"GLOBUL DOMINA..."

WHAT THE *HEY?*

TODAY'S GLOBEX!

HEALTH-FOOD MARKETING
NOVELTY SINGING FISH PRODUCTION
OSMOND SOUND-ALIKE RECORDING
BULK HYMNAL DISTRIBUTION
MAIL-ORDER WEDDING APPAREL

GLOBUL DOMINASHUN!

GENERAL CLAW, YOU *NUTBALL!*

TODAY'S GLOBEX!

HEALTH-FOOD MARKETING
NOVELTY SINGING FISH PRODUCTION
OSMOND SOUND-ALIKE RECORDING
BULK HYMNAL DISTRIBUTION
MAIL-ORDER WEDDING APPAREL

GLOBUL DOMINASHUN!

TEE-HEE!

THERE YOU ARE, SCORPIO! I'M HERE TO PUT AN **END** TO YOUR REIGN OF TERROR **ONCE AND FOR ALL!**

RRIIP!

OH, **GREAT.** AGENT JAMES BONT, AGAIN! JUST AS I'M INTERVIEWING OUR NEW **JOB APPLICANT!**

NOW, **EXPLAIN** THIS TO ME, GENERAL CLAW. DID YOU **TIE HIM UP** OVER THE **PIT OF ALLIGATORS**, LIKE I ASKED, WITH JUST A **SMALL CANDLE**...

...TO BURN SLOWLY THROUGH THE **ROPE**-- YES, I DID, MASTER, JUST AS YOU SAID!

WELL, **THIS** IS A FINE HOW-DO-YOU-DO!

HIS CONTINUED EXISTENCE FILLS ME WITH **SHAME,** MASTER!

POW!

BAM!

BASH!

HEY, NOW, ENOUGH WITH THAT "MASTER" TALK! THERE'S NO **"TEAM"** IN **MASTER!**

NOW WE'RE TALKIN'!

ACTUALLY, IF YOU RE-ARRANGE THE LETTERS AND REMOVE THE "R" AND THE "S"...

OKAY, I CONFESS, WE STILL **DABBLE** IN HOLDING THE WORLD HOSTAGE, JUST A BIT, BUT YOU'LL BARELY **NOTICE** IT.

IT'S A VERY **COMPETITIVE** FIELD!

THE **GLOBEX** CORPORATION
WE DOMINATE BECAUSE WE *CARE!*

Dr. Nick Riviera IN
CRIME FAMILY PRACTICE

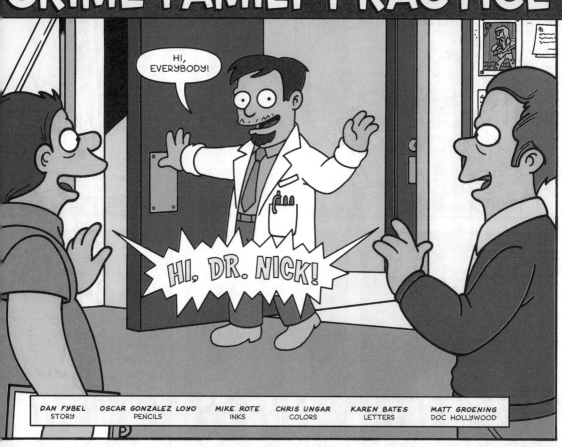

HI, EVERYBODY!

HI, DR. NICK!

DAN FYBEL	OSCAR GONZALEZ LOYO	MIKE ROTE	CHRIS UNGAR	KAREN BATES	MATT GROENING
STORY	PENCILS	INKS	COLORS	LETTERS	DOC HOLLYWOOD

THANKS FOR FILLING IN ON SUCH *SHORT NOTICE*. WAIT A MINUTE, AREN'T YOU THE GUY THAT WAS JUST IN THE BATHROOM STEALING TOILET PAPER?

WHAT DO YOU SAY WE TAKE SOME CALLS? LINE ONE, YOU'RE ON WITH *DR. NICK* AND SOME *STRANGE COMEDIAN!*

HELLO? I HAVEN'T *BURPED* IN FIVE HOURS. AM I *DYING*?

YES, YOU ARE. WHY NOT COME TO MY CLINIC FOR A *LOOKSEE*? HOW'S *TUESDAY AT NOON*?

:BRAAP!: I'LL BE THERE!

MY INCREDIBLY HIGH FEE WILL MAKE HIM FORGET HIS CERTAIN DEATH. DID I JUST SAY THAT *ON THE AIR*?

YOU EVER *BURP* AND *SNEEZE* AT THE *SAME TIME*? NOW, WOULD THAT BE A "*SNURP*" OR A "*BNEEZE*"? THE FUNNY THING ABOUT SNEEZING IS--

LINE TWO, I AM HERE TO MAKE YOU HEALTHY!

AN HOUR LATER...

WHAT A WONDERFUL FEELING TO HELP PEOPLE. OKAY, SEE YOU AGAIN WHEN MY *APPOINTMENT BOOK* LOOKS SKINNY!

THAT REMINDS ME OF THE TIME MY BUDDY, EARL, THE ONE WITH THE TURTLES--

GOODBYE, MR. RADIO MAN!

NOW WHERE DID I PARK MY *WHEEL THINGY*?

OH, *HERE* SHE IS!

NAB!

HELLO, DR. NICK.

ULP...HELLO, EVERYBODY.

I'LL CUT TO THE CANNOLI. YOU NEED *NEW PATIENTS* AND MY "FAMILY" NEEDS A *NEW DOCTOR*.

YOU'RE IN LUCK. I CAN MAYBE SQUEEZE YOU IN, SAY...FEBRUARY?

OR PERHAPS, SAY...*RIGHT NOW*?!

SOON...

I GOT YOUR CUSTOMERS RIGHT HERE, PALLY!

DR. NICK

BRIBERY ILLUSTRATED

EXTORTION DIGEST

WOULD YOU MIND KINDLY REMOVING THESE *SHOES* FOR ME? THEY'RE NOT MY SIZE, AND FRANKLY, I'M NOT SO FOND OF *THE STYLE*.

NURSE, MY JACKHAMMER! *NEXT*!

I WAS HOLDING A DOOR OPEN FOR A DEAR OLD LADY. IT WAS AN ESPECIALLY *HEAVY* DOOR.

LATER...

BOY, OH BOY. I *NEVER* WORK *THIS* MANY MINUTES IN A ROW. TIME FOR A NAP.

DR. NICK. PERHAPS YOU COULD BE OF ASSISTANCE.

HOLY HEMOGLOBIN, WHAT HAPPENED TO *YOU*?

OH THIS? YOU KNOW HOW *PLAYFUL* POLICE DOGS CAN GET SOMETIMES.

GRRR

GRRR

K-9

ALL THAT *RED STUFF*...OH, I'M STARTING TO FEEL A LITTLE *WOOZY*.

DR. NICK, I SUGGEST YOU QUICKLY GET OVER YOUR *SQUEAMISHNESS,* OR YOU WILL BE PERFORMING *EMERGENCY SURGERY* TO REMOVE MY BRUNO MAGLI SHOE FROM THE CRACK OF YOUR--

GRRR

OKAY, ALL RIGHT, LET ME THINK BACK TO MY DAYS OF ARDUOUS STUDY AT THE MEDICAL SCHOOL...

GRRR

GRRR

GRRR

"I MUST HAVE LEARNED *SOMETHING* ABOUT DOGS..."

HAIR OF THE DOG...

NO, THAT'S NOT IT.

EXCUSE ME, DR. NICK?

GRRR

GRRR

GRRR

...THEN THE COURSE *DOGLEGS* TO THE LEFT AFTER THAT *SAND TRAP.*

WILL ANY OF THIS BE ON THE *BIOMETRY TEST,* PROFESSOR?

NOPE. THAT DOESN'T SEEM TO HELP EITHER.

HEY, DOC...

GRRR

GRRR

GRRR

GROWING PAINS!

DAD! YOU'RE WIPING YOUR BIG, DUMB FACE WITH MY Z-MEN COMIC!

GAIL SIMONE	PHIL ORTIZ	TIM BAVINGTON	ART VILLANUEVA	KAREN BATES	MATT GROENING
STORY	PENCILS	INKS	COLORS	LETTERS	MR. GREEN JEANS

NOW, BART, I HAVE IN MY POCKET FOUR SHINY QUARTERS. YOU CAN GO AND BUY *SEVERAL* NEW COMICS, AND MAYHAP A *FESTIVE PENNYWHISTLE*, AND STILL HAVE TUPPENCE REMAINING!

THAT COMIC COST *$7.50*, HOMER.

D'OH!!

LISA! BART! I THINK I HAVE A WAY TO SOLVE *BOTH* YOUR PROBLEMS, EVEN THOUGH I'VE ALREADY FORGOTTEN WHAT LISA'S PROBLEM IS! TO THE *BASEMENT*, BOY!

WHEN *I* WAS A BOY, COMICS WERE MADE OF *FIBER-GLASS*, AND YOU HAD TO WEAR *SPECIAL GLOVES* TO READ 'EM! *"SCRATCHY DREADFULS,"* WE CALLED THEM.

SEE, BOY, YOUR OLD MAN'S A *THINKER!* NOT ONLY DID I *SAVE* THE VERY *FIRST* COMIC I EVER BOUGHT, BUT I EVEN *STORED* IT IN A PLASTIC BAG TO KEEP IT IN *MINT CONDITION!*

GUESS I SHOULDN'T HAVE USED A SANDWICH BAG. *ENJOY*, SON!

BUT, *DAD...!*

NOW, DON'T GO ALL *MILHOUSE* ON ME, BOY. THE LOOK IN YOUR EYES IS THANKS ENOUGH.

RASSA FRASSA STINKIN' DUMB OL' PIECE O' JUNK FUNNYBOOK, ANYWAY!

WELL, THAT'S ONE FAMILY CRISIS AVERTED IN MY OWN COMICAL STYLE. AND NOW, IT'S FINALLY *HOMER-TIME*. WHERE'S THAT REMOTE?

LET'S FACE IT, EVERY-ONE. IF WE DON'T THINK OF A WAY TO **RAISE** SOME FUNDS, WE'LL HAVE TO **SHUT DOWN** THE ENVIRO-BEARS FOR **GOOD!**

OOOH, I **HATE** GOATAL WARMING! IT MAKES LISA SAD!

WELL, WHAT IF, SAY, SOMEONE **ACCIDENTALLY** ROBBED A FEW GAS STATIONS, AND MAYBE THEY, **HYPO-THETICALLY,** "DONATED" THE PROCEEDS? **FIGURATIVELY SPEAKING,** I MEAN?

KEARNEY, THAT'S A LOVELY THOUGHT, BUT I DON'T THINK YOU SHOULD BREAK THE LAW TO SAVE OUR CLUB.

YOU FIGURED OUT THAT I MEANT **ME,** RIGHT?

RIGHT.

DANG!

KIDS, DON'T WORRY! I JUST THOUGHT OF THE GREATEST IDEA OF ALL TIME!

BETTER THAN PENICILLIN, MR. SIMPSON?

MOST PEOPLE **HATE** PENICILLIN, MILHOUSE. BUT **THIS** IDEA'LL RAISE A **TON** OF MONEY FOR YOUR CLUB!

NO, HOMER. NO **STREAK-A-THONS.** IT DIDN'T WORK FOR **MONDALE,** AND IT WON'T WORK NOW.

D'OH.

SORRY TO BREAK THIS UP, KIDS, BUT I'VE GOT A TRUNKFUL OF HARRY POTTER BOOKS TO **BURN** BEFORE ANY CHILDREN DISCOVER THE JOY OF READING...

OOOH! IT'S A DOUBLE-FEATURE, KIDS! THE REVEREND'S GONNA DO SOME OL' FASHIONED **BOOK-COOKIN'!**

HOORAY!

Harry Potter and the Sorcerer's Kidney Stone

I HAVE MY **SCHOOL BOOKS** IN THE CAR!

EVERYONE TRY TO THINK OF A MONEY-RAISING IDEA BEFORE NEXT WEEK'S MEETING, OKAY?

OH, SWEETIE, I'M SURE YOU'LL THINK OF SOMETHING.

YEAH, LIKE WHEN **JERRY LEWIS** BUSTED UP WITH **DEAN MARTIN.** HE WAS SO SAD, HE WENT RIGHT OUT AND INVENTED PENICILLIN!

ONE WEEK LATER...

SURELY THERE'S SOME *WACKY, MADCAP SCHEME* TO MAKE MONEY THAT WE HAVEN'T TRIED YET...

OH, WHO AM I KIDDING? I CAN'T EVEN GET PEOPLE TO CARE ABOUT SPRINGFIELD, OUR OWN HOMETOWN. I MIGHT AS WELL GIVE UP AND CALL THE OTHERS. ‡SIGH!‡

LISA, I'M GOING TO ASK YOU A FEW QUESTIONS, AND I NEED YOU TO BE HONEST WITH ME. FIRST, DID YOU KNOW THAT THE COST OF ILLEGAL CROSSBOWS HAS *SKYROCKETED* SINCE 1962?

BART...WHAT ARE YOU *TALKING* ABOUT?

NEVER MIND. DID YOU KNOW THAT DAD'S *CREDIT CARD* CHARGES **32%** INTEREST?

32%?!? ISN'T THAT *USURY?*

YOU'RE NOT HELPING, LIS...ONE MORE QUESTION...

BART, I DON'T LIKE THE SOUND OF THIS...

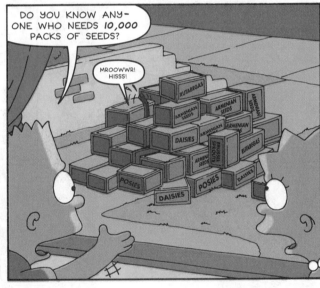

DO YOU KNOW ANY- ONE WHO NEEDS **10,000** PACKS OF SEEDS?

MROOWWR! HISSS!

RUTABEGAS
ARMENIAN SEEDS
ARMENIAN SEEDS
ARMENIAN SEEDS
DAISIES
ARMENIAN SEEDS
ARMENIAN
RUTABEGAS
POSIES
DAISIES
POSIES
DAISIES

BART, YOU'VE GOT TO MAKE THE SEED COMPANY TAKE THEM ALL BACK!

I TRIED THAT! THEY JUST *LAUGHED* AT ME!

I'M SO DEAD. TRY TO GET THEM TO SCATTER MY ASHES IN APU'S SQUISHEE MACHINE.

VIOLETS

I'VE *GOT* IT! WE'LL GET THE ENVIRO-BEARS TOGETHER, AND WE'LL SELL THEM! IT'LL BEAUTIFY THE TOWN, AND WHAT MONEY IS LEFT AFTER PAYING OFF DAD'S CREDIT CARD WILL GO INTO THE CLUB FUND!

SCAT! SCAT!

VIOLETS

¡AIEE! ¡PERO NÉCTAR ES *BUENO!*

BART, GET ME MY *LUCKY CLIPBOARD.*

‡GASP!‡

103

SOON...

ER, UH, I'M SORRY, LITTLE GIRL, BUT I'M AFRAID I'M *TOO BUSY* POLLING MY CONSTITUENTS TO BUY YOUR, UH, COOKIES, OR WHATEVER...

TEE HEE!

MISS CONGENIALITY

SAMPLES

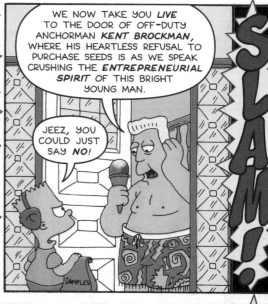

WE NOW TAKE YOU *LIVE* TO THE DOOR OF OFF-DUTY ANCHORMAN *KENT BROCKMAN*, WHERE HIS HEARTLESS REFUSAL TO PURCHASE SEEDS IS AS WE SPEAK CRUSHING THE *ENTREPRENEURIAL SPIRIT* OF THIS BRIGHT YOUNG MAN.

JEEZ, YOU COULD JUST SAY *NO*!

SAMPLES

SORRY, LI'L LISA, BUT I'M AFRAID I CAN'T BEAUTIFY MY GARDEN ANY MORE...I'M WALKING A *FINE LINE* BETWEEN GOOD CITIZENSHIP AND PRIDEFUL-NESS AS IT IS!

SAMPLES

DEFINE IRONY: A PRECOCIOUS TOT ATTEMPTING TO PROFIT OFF OF *ME*, INSTEAD OF T'OTHER WAY 'ROUND.

DOES THAT MEAN YOU'LL BUY SEEDS?

NO! FREAKIN' *KIDS!*

MAY THE FORCE BE WITH

AMPLES

DOES YA HAVE ANY SKUNKY-CABBAGE, BLACK-EYED KUDZU, OR MAMA'S TEAT-MILKWEED?

UH, NO. WE HAVE BEGONIAS, THOUGH!

I CAIN'T FEED NO *BEGONIAS* TO MY FAMILY. THAT'S *DISGUSTIN'*!

WHOA, MAN! YOU HAVE *SEEDS*? WHERE WERE YOU FIFTEEN MINUTES AGO?

AMPLES

30-40-41-42...THAT'S IT, GANG. EIGHT DOLLARS AND FORTY-TWO CENTS IS ALL WE COLLECTED.

DON'T FORGET THAT *FIVE* OF THOSE DOLLARS CAME FROM AUNT PATTY IN RETURN FOR ME WEARING THIS *STUPID SAILOR SUIT* ALL DAY!

MY PRIDE AND TOES HURT.

WELL, I COLLECTED OVER *FORTY DOLLARS* IN THE SCHOOL CAFETERIA ALONE!

KEARNEY! THAT'S *WONDERFUL!* HOW DID YOU EVER...?

HEY, I CAN'T HELP IT IF SOME OF THE SMALLER AND MORE-EASILY-INTIMIDATED KIDS WANTED TO CONTRIBUTE THEIR LUNCH MONEY!

WELL, EVEN WITH ALL THOSE KIDS GOING HUNGRY, WE STILL AREN'T ANYWHERE NEAR OUR GOAL...

I'LL GET IT! IT MIGHT BE A LOST PIZZA DELIVERY BOY OR A DANGEROUSLY OVERLOADED GYRO TRUCK!

KNOCK! KNOCK!

KRACKA-BOOOM!!!

GASP!

AH, HELLO, CHILDREN. SELLING...*SEEDS*, I SEE. WELL, I'VE COME TO ASK YOU TO STOP IT. NO, I'VE COME TO DEMAND THAT YOU CEASE YOUR SEED-SELLING THIS INSTANT!

STOP SELLING SEEDS? BUT WHY, MR. BURNS?

LET ME MAKE THIS VERY CLEAR, CHILDREN. I AM *ALLERGIC* TO GROWING THINGS. DO YOU THINK I BUILT THE MOST TOXIC *NUCLEAR PLANT* IN THE COUNTRY ON ACCIDENT? *PISH TOSH!*

SO YOU WILL DESIST YOUR PETTY *SEED-SELLING TOM-FOOLERY* AT *ONCE!* FOR IF YOU DO NOT...

...I WILL TAKE *DRASTIC* MEASURES! YOU HAVE BEEN *WARNED.*

HMMM. DO YOU THINK I CAME ON A LITTLE STRONG WITH THOSE TYKES, SMITHERS?

NOT AT ALL, SIR! IT WAS A *MASTERFUL* PERFORMANCE!

EXCELLENT. I'D HATE TO THINK I FRIGHTENED THEM, BUT JUST IN CASE THEY DIDN'T LISTEN, BETTER WARM UP THE *DEATH RAY*.

RIGHTI-O, SIR!

SOON...

MARGE! THOSE SURLY ARMENIANS ARE REPOSSESSING OUR *HOUSE*!

IT'S JUST LIKE THAT PSYCHIC HOTLINE PREDICTED! HOMER, *STOP THEM*!

ARMENIAN SEEDS HOUSE REPO. CO.

ALL YOU HAVE TO DO IS PAY THIS *SEED BILL*, THEN YOU GET THE BITS OF YOUR HOUSE BACK.

FIFTEEN THOUSAND DOLLARS!???!?! BUT I DIDN'T EVEN *ORDER* ANY SEEDS!

FIRST STEP IS ADMITTING YOU HAVE A PROBLEM, MISTER.

IF YOU DON'T PAY BY *MIDNIGHT TOMORROW*, WE'LL BE BACK FOR THE *REST*.

DAD...IT'S MY FAULT. I WANTED A CROSSBOW. I DIDN'T KNOW *THIS* WAS GONNA HAPPEN! I'M SORRY, DAD...:SNIFF!:

HOMEY, WHAT ARE WE GOING TO *DO*? WE CAN'T LOSE OUR *HOUSE*!

IN MY DAY, WHEN THERE WAS A MONEY CRISIS, THE WHOLE *TOWN* WOULD GET TOGETHER AND HAVE AN OLD-FASHIONED *COUNTRY FAIR*!

THAT'S A GREAT IDEA, GRAMPA!

THAT'S THE DUMBEST THING I'VE EVER HEARD.

ON THE OTHER HAND, A TOWN FAIR IS THE BEST IDEA *EVER*!

BETTER THAN *PENICILLIN*?

WHAP!

FRED

HMM. A *"TOWN FAIR,"* IS IT? WE'LL JUST SEE ABOUT *THAT*, MY MIDDLE CLASS FRIEND!

K-TEL'S Death Ray

LIP-READING FOR DUMMIEZ

THE NEXT DAY...

HEY, GUYS! CAN I COUNT ON YOU BOTH TO COME TO THE BIG TOWN FAIR TONIGHT?

MR. BURNS AIN'T GONNA BE TOO *HAPPY* WITH ANY OF HIS WORKERS GOIN' TO YOUR *FAIR* THERE, HOMER.

UMM...

WHAT? WHY DO YOU SAY THAT?

WELL, MAINLY ON ACCOUNTA THIS SIGNED DOCUMENT.

Notice of Intimidation

To all Plant Employees,

Regarding the so-called "Town Fair":
Anyone caught attending this repulsive tractor pull/hog-calling contest shall be soundly beaten and then dismissed, or otherwise harassed by thugs, and not those nice thugs shown in many delightful gangster comedies, either. That is all.

Sincerely,

C. Montgomery Burns

OH, SO YOU GUYS CAN'T DO ANYTHING WITH-OUT MR. BURNS' *APPROVAL* NOW, IS THAT IT? WHAT IS HE, YOUR *MOMMY* OR SOMETHING?

HEY, THAT'S NOT *FAIR!* YOU WORK FOR MR. BURNS, *TOO*, YOU KNOW!

WHAT'S THE MATTER, LENNY? CAN'T TAKE THE *HEAT* WHEN *MOMMY MCBURNS* ISN'T AROUND?

YEP. YOUR MOMMY IS A *WITHERED OLD MAN*. IN YOUR *FACE*, CARL!

QUIT SAYING THAT, HOMER. IT'S DISTURBING!

HOMER SIMPSON SEEMS TO BE AGITATING YOUR WORKER BEES IN *SECTOR 7-G*, SIR.

REALLY? WELL, NOTHING OILS THE *MACHINERY OF CAPI-TALISM* LIKE *SPIRITED DEBATE*, YOU KNOW! BEST OF LUCK TO THAT *RABBLE-ROUSING BEATNIK!*

SHALL I HAVE HIM *BEATEN*, SIR?

OH, YES. *THRICE*, I'D SAY!

GOD *BLESS* THE FALL OF THE *SOVIET SECRET POLICE*. THESE BRIGHT YOUNG CHAPS COST ABOUT A *THIRD* OF WHAT *MAFIA* KNEE-BREAKERS NORMALLY CHARGE!

FFFSSSHHH!

CLICK!

109

SMITHERS! WHERE ARE THOSE GAY LIGHTS AND MERRY SOUNDS COMING FROM? THE TOWN SQUARE? SURELY THEY'RE NOT HAVING THEIR CURSED "FAIR" AGAINST MY WISHES?

AH...IT APPEARS SO, MR. BURNS!

HEY, MOE! HOW'S BUSINESS?

UH, NOT TOO GOOD THERE, LISA. EVEN WITH THE FREE SEEDS I AIN'T SEEIN' NO ACTION. I CAN'T FIGURE IT NO HOW!

Kissing Booth

Come and get him, ladies! Only 2 dollars!

KRAZY KAJUN SEED-FILLED FRITTERS

OH, GOOD LORD!

OH, RIGHT! THE FACE! I FORGOT MY UGLY FACE AN' ALL! NOW DON'T THAT BEAT EVERYTHING?

AAIIIEEE!

AND HEY, AIN'T YOU SUPPOSED TO BE OVER AT THE GAZEBO? THEY BEEN LOOKIN' ALL OVER FOR YOU...SCOOT ALONG NOW OR THE FLAG WILL BE ROOINED!

BUT I HAVEN'T SEEN THE FAIR YET!

HEAR YE, HEAR YE! COME ONE AND ALL! COME AND WITNESS THE ETERNAL STRUGGLE OF MAN AND NATURE IN A GRIM TABLEAU OF SURVIVAL AGAINST THE ODDS!

AYE, BOSUN! I'LL MEET YER SALTY CHALLENGE! 'TIS A GOODLY CLOWN-DUNKIN' I FORSEE!

HEY, HEY! LOOK EVERY-ONE! POPEYE HERE THINKS HE'S GOING TO PUT THE CLOWN IN THE WATER! GIVE ME YOUR BEST SHOT, AHAB!

WHIFF!

MISS!

DUNK A CLOWN! AND GET FREE SEEDS! FREE BALLS—$5!

KZZAAAAPPP!

RUMBLE!

RUMBLE!

LOOK OUT!

¡GASP!

KA-BOOM!!

KA-BOOM!!

IS THIS THE END OF YE OLDE MILHOUSE?!

¡YO-YOIKS!¡ THAT *BEAM* COMING FROM THE *POWER PLANT* IS MAKING THOSE *IRRADIATED SEEDS* HIGHLY UNSTABLE WITH THE *BLOWING* AND THE EXPLOSIVE-TYPE *KABOOM-ING!*

BAM!

WELL, THANK YOU, MR. *EXPOSITION.*

UH, I'M AFRAID THE DEATH RAY IS SOMEHOW *MASSIVELY ACCELERATING* THE SEEDS' GROWTH, MR. BURNS!

DRAT. IT'S LIKE *NICARAGUA* ALL OVER AGAIN.

LOOK OVER THERE!

THE SEEDS ARE GROWING LIKE CRAZY! IT'S *BEAUTIFUL!*

SPRINGFIELD COUNTY COURT HOUSE

AW, WILL YOU LOOK AT THE LOVELY COLORS! I FEEL SO *RENEWED!*

I CAN *TASTE* IT WITH MY *SNIFF-SNIFF!*

POLICE

POLICE

ARR, 'TIS A *TREE-BOAT* I HAVE NOW, I SEES. HANDSOME PETE AND I WILL BE BUNKIN' IN A PLACE OF *FLOWERY BEAUTY*, 'TIS TRUE.

CURSED ALLERGIES! QUICKLY, SMITHERS BRING ME MORE *POLLEN-FREE OXYGEN!*

YES, SIR!

OXYGEN

LOOK, MOM! WE RAISED *MORE* THAN ENOUGH MONEY TO PAY BART'S SEED BILL, AND WE BEAUTIFIED THE *WHOLE TOWN!*

OH, I'M SO *PROUD* OF YOU, SWEETIE!

YEAH, LIS...THANKS FOR SAVIN' MY BACON!

THE IMPORTANT THING IS WE GOT OUR *TOILET* BACK, AND NO ONE'S IN *JAIL.*

GOOD *LORD!* OUR TESTS INDICATE THAT THE RAY NOT ONLY MADE THE PLANTS GROW, IT MADE ALL THE ADULTS IN TOWN *INFERTILE!*

BEEP! BEEP!

HUH?

WHAT HE'S SAYING IS THAT NONE OF THE *GROWN-UPS* IN SPRINGFIELD CAN HAVE BABIES EVER AGAIN WITH THE *DIAPERS* AND THE *SMELLING* AND THE, *OH,* THOSE STRAINED PEAS!

BOOT! BOOT!

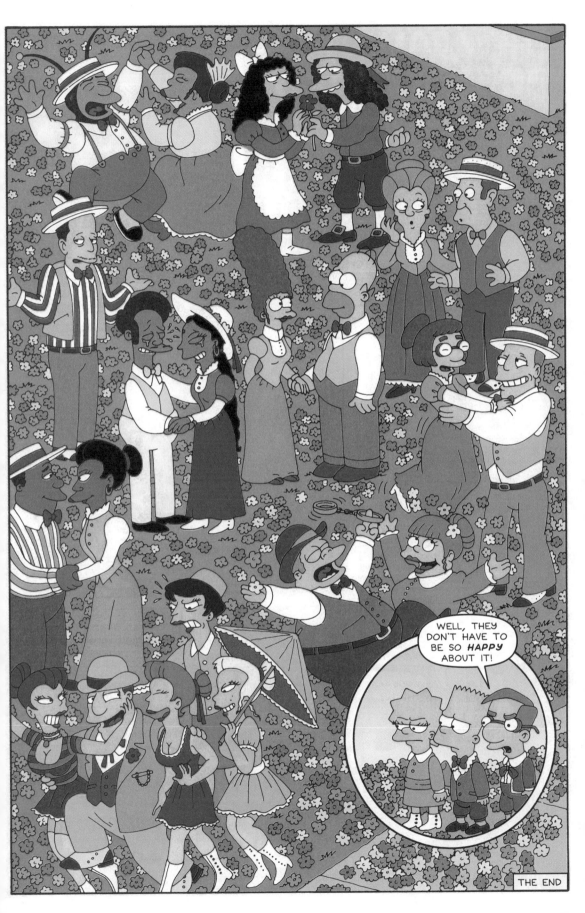

WELL, THEY DON'T HAVE TO BE SO *HAPPY* ABOUT IT!

THE END

WE'LL ALL MISS YOU!

YEAH, BEST OF LUCK ON THE OUTSIDE, DOC. SINCERELY.

BYE, DOC!

WE ♥ KOLAWSUS!

BAH! YOU'LL PAY FOR YOUR *INSOLENCE* WITH *COLOSSUS-INFLICTED DOOM!*

I JUST WANT TO SAY, DOCTOR, THAT IT'S BEEN MY *PLEASURE* TO HAVE BEEN YOUR WARDEN HERE THESE LAST THREE YEARS. GOOD LUCK TO YOU!

BAH! COLOSSUS CARES *NOT* FOR YOUR DEMEANING WORDS! *LEAVE AT ONCE,* OR *BE ANNIHILATED!*

AWW, WE'LL MISS YOU, TOO, YA BIG LUG.

¡SNIFF!¡

DR. COLOSSUS NEEDS *NO ONE!* YOU SHALL ALL BE *CRUSHED* UNDER THE *CRUSHING*...UH... *CRUSH POWER*...

...OF MY MIGHTY...ER... *CRUSHING BOOTS!*

YOU WILL *BEG* AND *PLEAD,* BUT *COLOSSUS* WILL *SHOW NO MERCY!*

COLOSSUS NEEDS A *RIDE* INTO *TOWN!*

HA! DESPITE YOUR STERNLY-WORDED SIGNS, I WILL *NEVER* USE EXACT CHANGE! *NEVER!*

THE *EVIL* OF COLOSSUS KNOWS *NO BOUNDS!*

DEATH MOUNTAIN

YEAH, OKAY, WHATEVER.

119

NOW...IF I CAN ONLY REMEMBER WHERE THE *LIGHT SWITCH OF TORMENT* IS LOCATED.

I HOPE THOSE *BATS* DON'T ATTACK ME LIKE *LAST* TIME...

KLICK!

ACK! GAH! GURF!

FLAP! FLAP! FLAP! FLAP! FLAP!

SHORTLY...

MY *REVENGE* UPON THE WORLD THAT HAS SHUNNED ME *BEGINS* THIS VERY EVENING! BUT FIRST, I'LL NEED THE BOOTS FROM MY SPARE COSTUME!

ONLY THE GENIUS OF *COLOSSUS* COULD HAVE ENVISIONED SUCH *SHOES OF TYRANNY!*

SHISSSSSH!

PAF!

AH, THERE YOU ARE. MY BOOTS, MY *PRECIOUS* BOOTS.

DID YOU MISS ME?

DON'T WORRY. *DADDY'S HOME.*

AH-HAHAHA HAHAHA!

GAAAAAH!

FLAP! FLAP! FLAP! FLAP!

CAN'T YOU, I DON'T KNOW...*ARREST* HIM OR SOMETHING? HE'S BECOMING A *NUISANCE!*

WHAT, ARREST OL' DOC COLOSSUS? AWW...

"...YOU DON'T REALLY WANT ME TO ARREST THE POOR GUY, DO YA? I MEAN, LET'S FACE IT..."

"...HE'S *COMPLETELY* HARMLESS."

:SNIFF!:

THANKS FOR THE RIDE, EDDIE.

HEY, CHIN UP, DOC! I'M SURE YOU'LL BE BACK TA COMMITIN' MAJOR CRIMES WIT' DEM BOOTS O' YOURS ANY DAY NOW! YOU TAKE HER EASY, ALL RIGHT?

BAH.

THAT'S THE SPIRIT!

YOU HAVE *ONE* MESSAGE.

HELLO, DR. COLOSSUS? THIS IS *GENERAL KLAW* FROM THE *SECRET SOCIETY OF EVIL GENIUSES.* I'M AFRAID WE'VE VOTED TO *REVOKE* YOUR *MEMBERSHIP.* YOU'RE JUST TOO *EMBARRASSING.* CALL ME, WE'LL PLAY *BRIDGE* SOMETIME.

:SIGH.:

IT'S TRUE. IT'S *ALL TRUE.* COLOSSUS *IS* A FAILURE AS A CRIMINAL MASTERMIND!

ALL I WANT IS TO CAUSE PEOPLE TO *FLEE IN TERROR*...IS *THAT* TOO MUCH TO ASK?

FLAP!
FLAP!
FLAP!
FLAP!

AACCK! :SPUTTER!: GAH! FILTHY CREATURES!

ONE WEEK LATER...

UH...IQ OF 203, ADVANCED DEGREES IN *CHEMISTRY* AND *PHYSICS*...

I JUST WANT THE JOB WITH THE *LEAST* RESPONSIBILITY.

I'M AFRAID YOU'RE JUST *TOO* OVER-QUALIFIED, MR. COLOSSUS, SIR! EVEN THE *HEAD FRY COOK* ONLY HAS A *BASIC MEDICAL DEGREE!*

ALL RIGHT, *BURGER-JOCKEYS!* THIS IS *TOTALLY* A *STICK-UP!*

BAH! AMATEUR!

TAP!

DUDE! I'M, LIKE, *HEADIN'* FOR A *HEMORRHAGE!*

SPROING!

CRASH!

SOON...

...DOCTOR COLOSSUS, A SELFLESS HERO, HAS SAVED AN *ENTIRE RESTAURANT* FROM A *BLOOD-THIRSTY* CRIMINAL!

IT WAS AN *ACCIDENT!* COLOSSUS IS *EVIL!* HAS THE WORLD GONE *MAD?!?*

WE LOVE YOU COLOSSUS, OH, YES WE DO, WE DON'T LOVE ANYONE, AS MUCH AS YOU!

CURSE YOUR *FOOLISH LOVE* FOR *COLOSSUS!* I *DESPISE* YOU ALL!!!

DR. COLOSSUS
SPRINGFIELD'S GREATEST HERO!

AND THERE HE GOES, FOLKS. THE MOST *HUMBLE,* THE MOST *HEROIC* MAN I'VE EVER KNOWN.

HE WAS THE *BEST EMPLOYEE* WE *ALMOST* EVER HAD!

SNIFF!

GAIL SIMONE
STORY

JOHN COSTANZA
PENCILS

PHYLLIS NOVIN
INKS

RICK REESE
COLORS

KAREN BATES
LETTERS

COLOSSO-BOOTS SUPPLIED BY
MATT GROENING

ELSEWHERE... GOT A SHIPMENT OF RADIOACTIVE MAN'S HERE!

UH...I'LL SIGN FOR THOSE!

THE HAPPY LITTLE ELVES

HEH, HEH!

WAIT! WAIT! CURSE MY NEED TO VISIT THE "DANGER ROOM" EVERY TEN MINUTES!

I BLAME YOU, EXTRA LARGE MOUNTAIN DEW!

YEAH, I HEAR YA! SHOPLIFTING IS A TERRIBLE THING, BUT I'M AFRAID I'M HELPLESS TO DO ANYTHING!

HEY, LOU! THE CHIEF'S FALLEN ON HIS BACK AGAIN!

HE'S SO CUTE WHEN HE DOES THAT!

HEY, GUYS! LITTLE HELP?

LATER...

A BAG OF PORK RINDS, APU, MY GOOD MAN!

HERE YOU ARE, MR. HOMER, SIR!

THAT WILL BE $400

I TAKE IT BY THE TEX AVERY-STYLE UNHINGING OF YOUR JAW THAT YOU ARE SURPRISED BY OUR NEW PRICES.

I AM AFRAID SHOP-LIFTING HAS CAUSED ME TO GO FROM SIMPLE GOUGING TO A SUPER ULTRA-GOUGE.

IF *YOU*, THE CITY, WILL FUND *US*, THEN *WE SHOPKEEPERS* WILL *DEFEND OURSELVES* BY *TAKING THE LAW INTO OUR OWN HANDS.*

THE *POLICE* WON'T HAVE TO LIFT *ONE FAT FINGER!*

WILL THIS BE...ER...COOL CHARLES BRONSON-STYLE *VIGILANTE JUSTICE?*

YES!

MAN, I REALLY *HAVE* BEEN LETTING *MY FINGERS* GO.

FUNDING GRANTED!

HOORAY!

LATER, IN NED'S FLANDERS' BASEMENT...

WE ARE NOW A *LEAGUE OF EXTRA-ORDINARY GENTLEMEN* FIGHTING FOR TRUTH, JUSTICE, AND THE CAPITALIST WAY! WE NEED A *CATCHY NAME* TO *CONVEY FEAR* AND *RESPECT!*

I PROPOSE "*THE MERCHANTS OF VENGEANCE*"!

THAT'S A TAD *TOO VIOLENT* FOR MY TASTES. AND *VENGEANCE* IS ALREADY *SOMEONE ELSE'S* DEPARTMENT.

HOW ABOUT *JUSTICE FOR JESUS?*

UM...*NO!*

ANTI-PUNK PATROL!

THE HOLY HELPERS!

CAPTAIN COMIC BOOK AND HIS ALL-STAR SHOPKEEPERS!

131

SOON, THE CLERK CRUSADERS PUT THEIR PLAN INTO ACTION, WITH CUTTING EDGE GADGETRY!

MAN, APU'S NEVER AROUND. THIS IS *TOO EASY*, MAN.

CLICK!

CHUTN

WHAT'S UP WITH THE NOZZLE?

YAAAA!

FWOOOOOOSH!

I MUST SAY, YOUNG DOLPH, FOR ONE ABOUT TO BE ARRESTED FOR SHOP-LIFTING YOU CERTAINLY KNOW HOW TO *KEEP YOUR COOL*.

"KEEP YOUR COOL." HEH, HEH. I MUST SUBMIT THAT TO THE *KWIK-E-MART NEWSLETTER*'S "HUMOR AT WORK" SECTION.

MEANWHILE...

WHOA, A LEFT-HANDED COMB! THAT'D BE GREAT FOR HAIR-RELATED GROOMING!

TIME FOR A *FOUR-FINGER DISCOUNT.*

ALERT! ALERT! INITIATING LIVE VIDEO FEED!

JIMBO!

WE'RE SO *DISAPPOINTED!*

MOM! GRANDMA! NO! THIS CAN'T BE HAPPENING!

WELL, THERE'S ONE *FINGER WAGGING* THAT LAD WON'T SOON FORGET.

:SOB!:

SALE

AND...

I THINK YOU WILL FIND THE COMICS YOU ATTEMPTED TO STEAL WERE *PRE-TREATED* TO DELIVER TEN TIMES MORE *PAPER CUTS* THAN THE LEADING BRAND!

AAAH!

GAH!

NOW, ARE YOU GOING TO TURN YOURSELVES OVER TO THE *PROPER AUTHORITIES,* OR DO I HAVE TO BRING OUT...

...*THE LEMON JUICE?*

AAAH! NO MAN! PUT THAT THING AWAY!

WE'LL GO TO THE COPS RIGHT NOW! SEE, WATCH US GO!

AND SO *THE BETTER BUSINESS BATTALION* CONTINUED THEIR SHOPLIFTING CRUSADE. SUCCESS DOGPILED ON TOP OF SUCCESS.

HOLY MOSES!

AT THE TRY 'N' SAVE...

SPROING!

SHE WANTED TO STEAL AN ALBUM, BUT I THINK WE'VE MADE THAT MINISTER'S DAUGHTER *C.D. LIGHT!*

Inspirational Listening

AT A HOT DOG STAND...

LIKE, *WHAAAA!*

YOU WANTED A *WIENER,* BUT NOW YOU ARE A *LOSER,* SIR!

CLICK!

AND WITH THE DROP IN CRIME CAME BETTER PRICES FOR CONSUMERS.

BEER NOW SOLD FOR A QUARTER A GLASS!

LEADING HOMER TO GET SO DRUNK ONE NIGHT, HE AWOKE TO FIND...

THE NEXT DAY... WELCOME TO THE *TRYOUTS* FOR *NEW B.B.B. MEMBERS.* WE WILL CONDUCT THE TRIALS USING THE *LEGION OF SUPER- HEROES'* METHOD.

PRESENT WHAT YOU HAVE TO OFFER TO THE TEAM AND WE SHALL JUDGE YOU.

CAN WE TALK FOR ONE DIDDILY OF A SECOND?

LATER.

APU

NED

YES ○
NO ○

YES ○
NO ○

YES ○
NO ○

AAR! I'D BE *HONORED* TO JOIN YER CREW!

DIDN'T YOU *APPEAR* ON A BOX OF *POISONED FISH STICKS?*

AH, THERE'S A FUNNY STORY BEHIND THAT SENSELESS TRAGEDY!

NEXT!

WE DON'T WEAR COSTUMES.

OH THIS LITTLE NUMBER IS FOR A PARTY LATER. IT'S THE *ACTUAL SUIT* WORN BY *THE PUZZLER* IN THE 1960'S *RADIOACTIVE MAN TV SERIES.* ISN'T IT *THE LIVING END?*

SILVER AGE

SORRY, YOU'RE *TOO* CAMP!

NEXT!

I...

NEXT!

NOT *ONE* MET OUR *HIGH STANDARDS OF EXCELLENCE.* OH, WELL, WHAT SHALL WE DO TONIGHT *FELLOW CRIME FIGHTERS?*

YOU TELL HIM, MR. NED. WE AGREED YOU WOULD TELL HIM.

RARE COMICS

TELL ME WHAT? HEROES DON'T KEEP *SECRETS* FROM EACH OTHER.

APU

NED

IT'S JUST THAT THERE'S NO MORE CRIME. DAVID DIDN'T STICK AROUND AFTER HE BEAT GOLIATH.

WE'RE *NOT NEEDED* ANY- MORE.

BUT...THE GROUP. WHAT ABOUT *US*?

WE HAVE DONE OUR JOB, SIR.

YOU SHOULD BE AS *PROUD* AS IS ALLOWED WITHOUT IT BECOMING A SIN.

WE WISH TO *RETIRE* WITH *CLASS* AND *DIGNITY*, LIKE *THE BANGLES*, NOT OVER-STAY OUR WELCOME IN *SHAME*, LIKE *THE GO-GOS*.

IF THERE'S EVER *TROUBLE*, YOU KNOW WHERE TO FIND US.

GOODBYE. I SHALL STILL HONOR YOUR *B.B.B.* 10% *SQUISHEE DISCOUNT* UNTIL THE END OF THE MONTH.

BUT WHAT WILL I DO?

JUST GET BACK TO YOUR *LIFE*.

YES, JUST GET BACK TO MY LIFE.

138

THE NEXT WEEK...

THIS YOUNG SHOPLIFTER MUST HAVE THOUGHT IT WAS SAFE TO RETURN TO A LIFE OF CRIME!

BUT THAT WAS BEFORE HE MET *THE B.B.B. BUMPER STICKER BLASTER!*

THAT'S SOME NICE APPREHENDING, MR. G!

I JUST GOT THE GOOD WORD! YOU'VE CAUGHT *FIVE* SHOPLIFTERS IN JUST ONE WEEK.

I SUPPOSE WE WERE *TOO HASTY* IN BREAKING UP OUR GROUP.

THEN WE'RE BACK?

AS LONG AS SHOPLIFTERS THREATEN OUR COMMUNITY, WE'LL BE THERE.

HUZZAH!

UH, HUH! WELL, IF *I* WERE YOU, I'D JUST TELL AUSTRALIA TO EAT MY SHORTS.

BART! LISA! THE *SCHOOL BUS* IS HERE!

GOTTA GO, HOMER!

MAN, THE BUS SURE IS *EMPTY* TODAY.

EVERYONE'S BEEN *ARRESTED* FOR SHOPLIFTING. IT DOESN'T MAKE SENSE.

DOLPH, NELSON, KEARNEY I CAN SEE...

...BUT MILHOUSE? MARTIN? SHERRI AND TERRI?

WELL, TERRI I CAN SEE. *SHE'S* THE *EVIL TWIN*, RIGHT?

SOMETHING'S GOING ON, BART.

AW, YOU'RE JUST BEING *PARANOID*.

I HOPE SO.

LATER...

AH, NOTHING LIKE AN *AFTER SCHOOL SQUISHEE* TO WASH AWAY THE *BITTER TASTE OF LEARNING*.

NEW KRUSTY KARAMEL KRUNCH? *THIS* I GOTTA TRY.

BUY!

ALERT!

ALERT!

WHAT THE...?

GAAAH!

BANG!

CRUNCH!

I'VE BEEN *ACCUSED* OF A CRIME I DIDN'T COMMIT!

OH, GREAT, I'LL BET SOMEONE'LL BLAME IT ON THE *ONE-ARMED MAN* AGAIN!

MINUTES LATER...

AND THAT'S THE WHOLE STORY. I'M *INNOCENT* I TELLS YA!

I BELIEVE YOU, BART. BUT WE NEED *PROOF.*

DING! DONG!

IT'S *THEM!*

KEEP QUIET! NO ONE KNOWS YOU'RE HERE.

HELLO THERE, MARGE. SORRY TO BE A *BITHER-BOTHER,* BUT IS BART HOME?

NO, HE ISN'T.

NOW IT'S NOT THAT WE DON'T *TRUST* YOU, BUT...

...TURN IT ON FELLAS!

AYE CARUMBA!

MY WORD!

AHA! *THE BATTALION'S SUPER X-RAY-O-SCOPE* FLUSHES OUT THE *EVILDOER!*

RUN!!!

LEAP!

TO THE B.B.B.MOBILE!

WE'RE ALREADY IN IT!

THEN *ATOMIC BATTERY TO POWER* AND *TURBINES TO SPEED*, APU!

JUST DRIVE THE RV.

WHY DID YOU NOT SAY SO IN THE FIRST PLACE?

VROOOM! VROOOM!

WHERE DID THEY GO?

AUSTRALIA DECLARES WAR ON NEW ZEALAND

:GASP!:

:HUFF!: :PUFF!:

LISA, I DON'T WANT TO GET YOU IN TROUBLE, TOO. I'M GONNA TURN MYSELF IN.

OKAY!

OKAY? YOU'D LET ME TURN MYSELF IN? DON'T YOU KNOW A *BLUFF* WHEN YOU HEAR ONE? NOW HELP ME!

OKAY, OKAY! LET'S GO BACK TO *THE SCENE OF THE CRIME* AND LOOK FOR CLUES.

LATER...

THE KWIK-E-MART SHOULD BE CLOSED AS LONG AS APU'S LOOKING FOR YOU.

HERE'S THE SECURITY TAPE OF ME.

PUT IT IN!

ACHO CHEEZ™
Cheese Substitute

HMMMM...

YOU SEE SOMETHING?

MAYBE, I...

FREEZE!

IN THE WORDS OF THE BORG, "RESISTANCE IS FUTILE, PUNKS!"

WE'LL GO QUIETLY, BUT PLEASE JUST WATCH THE SECURITY TAPE ONE MORE TIME!

WELL, OKAY, BUT ONLY IF THERE ARE SNACKS.

SOON...

WATCH CAREFULLY.

HE'S AS GUILTY AS GREEDO!

LOOK CLOSER. THIS HAPPENED AFTER SCHOOL AROUND SUNSET. THERE'S THE SHADOW OF THE POTATO CHIP STAND.

WHERE'S *BART'S SHADOW?*

HE'S A *GHOST!*

¡GASP!¡

NOT A GHOST, BUT A *COMPUTER-GENERATED IMAGE* USED TO *FRAME* MY BROTHER!

THERE'S *NO PROOF* I DID IT!

LOOK IN THE LOWER LEFT CORNER OF THE SCREEN.

"BART SIMPSON FRAMING© B.B.B. VISIT OUR WEBSITE AT WWW.FRAMINGBART.ORG"

OKAY, OKAY I *CONFESS!*

YOU TOLD ME TO LIVE MY LIFE, BUT THIS GROUP *WAS* MY LIFE.

FOR THE *FIRST TIME EVER* I FELT *ACCEPTED,* EVEN, DARE I SAY IT... *LOVED.*

I WANTED TO BE A MARTIAN MANHUNTER, BUT I ENDED UP A HAL JORDAN.

I ONLY HOPE YOU CAN *FORGIVE* ME.

AW, HECK! *I'D* FORGIVE YOU EVEN IF THE BIBLE DIDN'T FORCE ME TO.

YOUR KARMA IS CLEAR WITH ME AS WELL.

WELL *I'M* STILL MAD!

THAT NON-FICTION *DISCOUNT BIN* IS A TOUGH MARKET TO CRACK!

REMAINDER

"ALL BOOKS 5¢"

I'LL TAKE ANOTHER *100 COPIES* FOR MY *KRUSTYBURGER* RESTAURANT.

OKAY, BUT UH...WHY?

ART

KIDS' BOOSTER SEATS ARE FIFTEEN DOLLARS EACH, AND THESE ARE THE *SAME SIZE* FOR A *NICKEL*.

DO THE MATH, STEPHEN HAWKING!

RT

A *SWEET VICTORY* INDEED. AND YET...I CRAVE *MORE*. SMITHERS, WHAT'S THE *BEST-SELLING BOOK OF ALL TIME*? WE'LL *CRUSH* THAT AUTHOR LIKE A *BUG*!

THAT WOULD BE *THE BIBLE,* SIR.

GAAHHH!

I TAKE IT WE WON'T BE DOING ANY *CRUSHING* TODAY?

NO, THIS CALLS FOR A SIMPLE CHANGE OF PLAN. IF YOU CAN'T BEAT THEM...

"...JOIN THEM!"

SPRINGFIELD CHURCH

NOW WITH 25% MORE DOGMA

AND IF THAT WASN'T BAD ENOUGH, THE *COLLECTION PLATE* IS BARER THAN J. LO'S MIDRIFF.

NED, YOU *ALONE* TITHE MORE THAN THIS!

SORRY, REVEREND. I INVESTED ALL MY SAVINGS IN *EVANGELICAL DOT COM STOCK*.

WE NEED *MONEY* PEOPLE! THIS PLACE NEEDS A LOT OF WORK!

REMEMBER WHEN BART SIMPSON SMASHED OUR STAINED GLASS WINDOWS OF THE APOSTLES AND WE CUT CORNERS BY HIRING LENNY TO REPLACE THEM? HE DID A FINE JOB BUT...

...THE CAST OF *"THE DREW CAREY* SHOW" WAS NOT WHAT I HAD IN MIND!

MAYBE IT'S *MY* FAULT THAT WE'VE LET THINGS GO AROUND HERE.

THREE HELLFIRE SERMONS ON TITHING PER MONTH MAY BE TOO MANY. PERHAPS A LITTLE MORE TIME SPENT ON THE FUNDAMENTALS WILL PRY OPEN YOUR POCKETBOOKS.

TELL YOU WHAT. I'M GOING TO OPEN THIS SERVICE UP TO ANY *QUESTIONS* YOU HAVE ABOUT THE *MYSTERIES OF OUR FAITH*.

I'VE GOT ONE! IF YOU DRINK HOLY WATER AND TAKE A WHIZ ON A VAMPIRE, WILL YOU KILL HIM?

WHAT NAME DOES GOD SCREAM WHEN HE STUBS *HIS* TOE?

WHY ARE THE PEARLY GATES ALWAYS *GOLD* IN CARTOONS WHEN PEARLS ARE OBVIOUSLY WHITE?

WHAT DOES THE H. IN "JESUS H. CHRIST" STAND FOR?

WHY AM I SEEN *SO FREQUENTLY* IN THIS CHURCH WHEN I AM CLEARLY *NOT* A CHRISTIAN?

HOW MUCH MONEY WILL IT TAKE TO *BUY* YOUR CHURCH?

¡GASP!¡

MR. BURNS!

I'M AFRAID THIS CHURCH IS *NOT FOR SALE!*

OH, THAT'S A PITY. REMOVE THE MONEY, SMITHERS.

BACK IN THE LIMOUSINE, SIR?

NO, THAT'S TOO MUCH TROUBLE. JUST *BURN IT* IN THE PARKING LOT.

WAIT! WHILE THE CHURCH ISN'T *FOR SALE*...

...THERE'S NOTHING IN THE BIBLE AGAINST...

...*SPONSORSHIP!*

EXCELLENT!

GOOD LORD, ;CHOKE!;

SOON...

EXODUS

I DON'T THINK I LIKE THE IDEA OF MR. BURNS SPONSORING THE CHURCH.

OH, MARGE! EVERYTHING HAS A SPONSOR. THE *BIG OIL COMPANIES* SPONSOR THE *GOVERNMENT* AND THAT'S ;COUGH; WORKED OUT ;HACK; FINE!

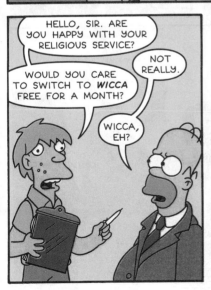

HELLO, SIR. ARE YOU HAPPY WITH YOUR RELIGIOUS SERVICE?

NOT REALLY.

WOULD YOU CARE TO SWITCH TO *WICCA* FREE FOR A MONTH?

WICCA, EH?

WE'RE HAPPY WITH OUR RELIGION, THANK YOU!

REMEMBER WHEN YOU BECAME A *MONK* FOR TWO MONTHS AFTER TALKING TO THAT *BUDDHIST*? I'M NOT GOING THROUGH *THAT* AGAIN.

THE NEXT WEEK...

AS YOU CAN SEE, THE STAINED GLASS WINDOWS HAVE BEEN *CHANGED*. MR. BURNS TELLS ME THIS IS JUST *TEMPORARY* AND THE APOSTLES ARE *ON ORDER*.

HEY, LOOK! THERE ARE ONLY *FIVE* COMMANDMENTS NOW!

≥WHEW!≤ THAT'S *WAY EASIER* TO REMEMBER.

REVEREND, MAY I SAY A FEW WORDS?

WELL, I...

TAKE FIVE, PADRE!

AS YOU CAN SEE, I'VE MADE A *FEW CHANGES*, AND I THINK YOU'LL *ENJOY* THEM.

HEY, EACH PEW HAS A *MAKE YOUR OWN TACO BAR*!

NOW THAT'S *GOOD RELIGION*!

ONE SMALL THING. IT'S NOW A *SIN* TO BELONG TO THE *FOLLOWING ORGANIZATIONS*...

...THE ENVIRONMENTAL PROTECTION AGENCY, GREENPEACE, AND LISA SIMPSON'S TREE HUGGING SOCIETY.

WHAT? WHY I...

QUIET, *SINNER!* LEST YE DAMN US ALL!

YOU SEE, CHURCH IS LIKE A *BOOK CLUB* WHERE EVERY WEEK THEY TALK ABOUT THE *SAME BOOK*.

WHAT WOULD *OPRAH* THINK ABOUT THAT?

NOW, THE BIBLE IS A FINE...

AHHHH! IT BURNS!

AS I WAS SAYING, THE BIBLE IS A *FINE BOOK*, BUT SO ARE OTHERS LIKE...

...WELL...*MY AUTOBIOGRAPHY* FOR ONE.

WE'LL TALK ABOUT THIS FOR A *MONTH OR TWO*...

...THEN MOVE ON TO THE *AYN RAND COLLECTION* AND *JOSEPH STALIN'S "HOW TO WIN FRIENDS AND CRUSH ENEMIES"*.

THIS IS *HORRIBLE!*

I KNOW. I'D LIKE TO *PROTEST*, BUT THE IDEA OF A *MANDATORY BOOK CLUB* IS JUST *TOO* APPEALING.

WELL I'VE HAD JUST ABOUT ALL I CAN STAND. ROD! TODD! *WE'RE LEAVING!*

FINE! GO!

BUT ONCE YOU LEAVE, *YOU CAN NEVER COME BACK!*

!

I'M WARNING YOU...

SOON...

SO YOU NEED A *NEW* RELIGION, HUH?

I FEEL SO *EMPTY* INSIDE.

THEN, BROTHER, YOU CAME TO THE RIGHT PLACE. IT'S GREAT BEING JEWISH!

THE FOOD'S GOOD, AND THERE'S *MORE HOLIDAYS* THAN YOU CAN SHAKE A STICK AT.

COME WITH ME!

I LOVED THE MATZO BALL SOUP AND THE KNISHES, BUT THIS PRODUCTION OF "FIDDLER ON THE ROOF" IS A BIT *DEPRESSING*.

IT'S THE *ORTHODOX VERSION*. THE DAUGHTERS ALL *LISTEN* TO THEIR FATHER, TEVYE, INSTEAD OF *REBELLING*.

BUT THEY ALL DIE *OLD MAIDS*.

C'MON, LET'S GET OUT TO THE SNACK TABLE BEFORE ALL THE KUGEL'S GONE!

WELL DONE.

EXCELLENT!

I PARTICULARLY ENJOYED THE *LACK OF DANCING*.

CLAP! CLAP! CLAP! CLAP! CLAP! CLAP!

YOUR LOSS.

BUT IF YOU CHANGE YOUR MIND, HERE'S A *COUPON* FOR A BUY-ONE-GET-ONE -FREE *BRIS*.

I DON'T KNOW. I JUST DON'T THINK THE SHOE FITS ME.

LATER...

THE LIFE OF A HINDU IS A *PEACEFUL* AND *FULFILLING* ONE!

WHAT? I CAN'T *HEAR* YOU OVER YOUR CRYING CHILDREN, THE CASH REGISTER, AND GUNFIRE!

WAAAAAH!

CH- CHING!

BANG!

BANG!

WAAA'A'!

DUDE! I'M LIKE TOTALLY IN A *RUSH*.

I SAID THE LIFE OF A HINDU IS A *PEACEFUL* AND *FULFILLING* ONE!

:SIGH!:

NO LOITERING!

POW!

Duff

OPEN

EVEN LATER...

YOU REALLY SHOULD CONSIDER *SNAKE HANDLING* AS YOUR NEW RELIGION!

HSSSSSSSS

AAAAAH!

HEY, NED, BE A PAL AND *CALL 911*, WOULD YA?

MAN, THE ONLY DAY I DON'T BRING *MY KNIFE* TO WORK!

HSSSSSSSSSSSSSS

LATER STILL...

I CAN OFFER YOU A RELIGION OF *BLISS* AND *CONTENTMENT*.

WELCOME TO KRUSTY BURGER

HEY, AM I PAYING YOU TO *CLEAN THE GREASE TRAPS* OR *RECRUIT* FOR YOUR *CULT*?

TO CLEAN THE TRAPS ...SIR!

WELCOME TO KRUSTY BURGER

:SIGH.:

OOOF!

AAAH! SORRY!

CRASH!

EASY THERE! WHAT'S THE SUN-DAY RUSH?

WE'RE *LATE* FOR CHURCH, AND THE MINISTER IS *AWFUL STRICT!*

STRICT YOU SAY?

IS THIS *OLD-TIME RELIGION?*

REALLY OLD, YEAH!

MIND IF I TAG ALONG?

AS LONG AS YOU DON'T MIND *LONG SERMONS* AND *HARD PEWS.*

THANK YOU, LORD!

MEANWHILE...

WILL *I* EVER GET TO TALK?

I DON'T KNOW. MR. BURNS IS REALLY *ENJOYING* THIS. HE EVEN BUYS HIS CLOTHES AT "THE HOUSE OF SHARPTON" NOW.

BROTHERS AND SISTERS. I HAVE A *PARABLE* FOR YOU!

LOOK AT THE VIDEO MONITOR IF YOU WILL.

THE MAN WHO PLANTED ATOMS

"ONCE UPON A TIME THERE WAS A MAN WHO PLANTED *ATOMS*."

"HE WOULD THROW THEM HITHER AND YON!"

"THE ATOMS THAT FELL ON THE *ROAD*..."

"...WELL, NOTHING HAPPENED."

"THE ONES THAT FELL ON *RICH SOIL*..."

"...THE SAME. NOTHING! ZIP! NADA!"

"BUT THE ATOMS THAT FELL IN A *WELL-MAINTAINED NUCLEAR FACILITY* SUPPLIED *CLEAN, EFFICIENT ENERGY* FOR *EVERYONE!*"

I'M CONFUSED.

YOU'RE SAYING OUR *SOULS* ARE LIKE ATOMS?

NO! NO! NO! NUCLEAR ENERGY IS THE *SOUL* OF *THIS TOWN!*

IT WAS A *SUBTLE ALLEGORY*. IF YOU NEED ME TO BE AS HAM-FISTED AS C.S. LEWIS, I WILL BE!

LATER...

MR. BURNS, I'M AFRAID THIS JUST ISN'T WORKING OUT.

I AGREE.

YOU DO? WELL, THAT'S A RELIEF. YOU SEE...

YOU'RE *FIRED*!

WHAT?!!

BUT YOU *CAN'T* FIRE ME!

I'VE PAID TO *RENOVATE* THE ENTIRE CHURCH IN THE LAST TWO WEEKS. THERE'S NOT AN *ORIGINAL* BRICK OR BOARD OF WOOD LEFT. I *OWN* THIS BUILDING. PLUS I'M BRINGING *THE CROWDS* IN!

YOU ARE *THE WEAKEST LINK. GOODBYE.*

I DON'T GET THAT AT ALL.

IT'S A LINE FROM A POPULAR TELEVISION PROGRAM.

I DON'T WATCH TV.

NOT EVEN *PBS?*

WELL, YES...PBS.

THEN YOU WATCH TV. I *HATE* WHEN PEOPLE SAY THAT!

OH, JUST *GET OUT!*

MEANWHILE...

WELL BOYS, HOW ARE YOU ENJOYING THE SERVICE?

I DON'T KNOW DADDY. SOMETHING SEEMS *WRONG*.

I MISS OUR OLD CHURCH.

I DO TOO, TODD, BUT THIS IS THE *NEXT BEST THING*.

WHY DOES HE HAVE A *GOAT'S HEAD* ON HIS CHEST?

GOATS ARE GOD'S CREATURES TOO, SON.

HE SURE TALKS ABOUT *THE DEVIL* A LOT.

YOU CAN'T WARN FOLKS TOO MUCH ABOUT HIM! WE MUST ALWAYS *BE ON GUARD.*

LATER...

HEY, LISA, WANT TO GET SOME *ICE CREAM?* MY TREAT.

BART, WHERE DID YOU GET THE MONEY?

REVEREND LOVEJOY'S *THREE CARD MONTE* GAME.

REVEREND LOVEJOY! WHAT ARE YOU DOING?

LOSING MY SHIRT.

I'M BROKE, AND I HEARD THAT THIS WAS SUPPOSED TO BE A *SURE-FIRE MONEYMAKER.*

ARE YOU *CHEATING?*

OF COURSE NOT. THAT WOULD BE *WRONG!*

LATER...

WE NEED YOU BACK AT THE CHURCH, REVEREND.

BUT EVERYONE ENJOYS MR. BURNS' SERMONS WITH HIS *INFOMERCIAL CARTOONS*.

THEY'RE GETTING *BORING* NOW.

COMMERCIALS ARE FUN *THE FIRST TIME*, BUT THEY GET OLD REALLY FAST.

CAN YOU HELP ME GET MY JOB BACK?

I'M GLAD YOU ASKED! WE HAVE A PLAN!

THAT NIGHT, OUTSIDE THE SPRINGFIELD COMMUNITY CHURCH...

I'VE GOT A *BAD* FEELING ABOUT THIS, CHILDREN...

BREAKING AND ENTERING JUST FEELS *WRONG* ...ESPECIALLY WHEN IT'S *GOD'S* HOUSE.

FELONIES ARE LIKE GETTING INTO AN *UNHEATED SWIMMING POOL*. DON'T THINK ABOUT IT AND JUMP RIGHT IN. YOU GET USED TO IT AFTER AWHILE.

LOOK AT *THIS* FILE! ≀GASP!≀

IT'S MR. BURNS' *MASTER PLAN*.

AAAAAH!

AHA! SMITHERS, ON MY WORD, PRESS THE BUTTON THAT BOTH *SUMMONS THE POLICE* AND EXCOMMUNI-CATES *THEM*!

YES, SIR!

ACCORDING TO THOSE FILES, YOU WERE USING MY CHURCH TO BECOME *POPE*?

IT STARTED WITH BOOSTING MY BOOK'S SALES, BUT THEN I GOT AN IDEA.

"LITTLE BY LITTLE I'D WORK MY WAY *UP THE LADDER*. ONE CHURCH AT A TIME UNTIL ONE DAY I WAS *POPE*."

"THEN I'D HAVE ACCESS TO ALL THE *VATICAN GOLD* AND *JEWELS*! AND IT'D ALL BE *TAX-FREE!*"

BUT THIS ISN'T A *CATHOLIC CHURCH*.

IT'S THE *SAME BIBLE*.

YES.

THE *SAME SAVIOR*?

YES.

BUT *NO POPE*?

NO.

SMITHERS WE'RE *LEAVING*. THIS RELIGION BUSINESS IS *MORE CONFUSING* THAN *THE INTERNET*.

YAY!

BUT FIRST, BEFORE I GIVE THE CHURCH BACK TO YOU, I'D LIKE YOU TO *INDULGE ME*.

CERTAINLY, WHAT CAN I DO?

AS I SAID. INDULGE ME. IN EXCHANGE FOR THE CHURCH BACK YOU'LL GIVE ME AN *INDULGENCE*.

YOU MEAN *BUY* YOUR WAY INTO *HEAVEN*? BUT THE CHURCH HASN'T DONE THAT IN *YEARS*.

IT'S STILL WITHIN YOUR *JURISDICTION*. I'VE MADE A *FEW ERRORS* IN MY TIME AND I NEED A *GUARANTEE* I'LL GET INTO HEAVEN WHEN I DIE.

JUST WRITE IT DOWN AND THE CHURCH IS *YOURS*.

EXCELLENT!

I'LL LEAVE A *COPY* FOR YOUR FILES AND BID YOU GOOD NIGHT!

OH MY SWEET LORD! IS THIS REALLY A CHURCH OF SATAN?

OF COURSE, IT IS! IT'S *WRITTEN* ON ALL OUR *STATIONERY*.

RUN BOYS, RUN!

WELL, WE *SCARED* ANOTHER ONE OFF. IS IT *ME*?

DON'T BEAT YOURSELF UP, ROY.

WHO WANTS TO MAKE *TOLL HOUSE COOKIES*?

AW! YOU GUYS ARE *THE BEST!*

LATER...

WELCOME BACK TO THE FLOCK, NED.

THANKS, REVEREND. IT FEELS LIKE *HOME!* ARE THE TACO BARS STILL HERE?

NO, BUT NOW IF EVERY-ONE PAYS ATTENTION, I SPRING FOR *PIZZA* AFTERWARDS.

WHAT ARE *YOU* DOING HERE?

I HEARD THERE WAS PIZZA.

A *FREE MEAL* IS A FREE MEAL.

JESSE McCANN AND ABBY DENSON
STORY

PHIL ORTIZ
PENCILS

PHYLLIS NOVIN
INKS

ART VILLANUEVA
COLORS

KAREN BATES
LETTERS

MATT GROENING
INTERIOR DECORATOR

OGDENVILLE...

HRMMM. *CLOSE* BUT NO CIGAR.

OGDENVILLE! *HAH!* THE PEOPLE HERE ARE SO *FULL* OF THEMSELVES! OOOH! I'M FROM OGDENVILLE! I AM *SOOO* SPECIAL!

OH, DEAR! PLEASE *EXCUSE* ME.

UUUH!

SEE WHAT I MEAN! THE PEOPLE HERE ARE *SO RUDE* WITH THEIR *HIGH* AND *MIGHTY OGDENVILLEAN ATTITUDES!*

OH, HUSH. WE WON'T BE HERE MUCH *LONGER!*

MAY I *HELP* YOU MISS?

YES. WE'RE LOOKING FOR FABRIC WITH A *CORNCOB* PATTERN.

COULD YOU PLEASE *WAIT* HERE A MOMENT? I'LL BE RIGHT BACK.

ANOTHER "*CONTACT*" IS HERE. SHE KNEW THE *CODE WORD*: "*CORNCOB*".

VERY GOOD. PROCEED WITH *PHASE TWO.*

YOUR *INSTRUCTIONS* ARE IN THIS ENVELOPE. IT CONTAINS ALL THE *INFORMATION* YOU NEED. YOU MUST *DESTROY* IT *IMMEDIATELY* AFTER READING IT.

OH, *MY!* CORN-COB FABRIC MUST BE GETTING *VERY* POPULAR!

THE END